I'LL ALWAYS REMEMBER

INSIDE THE MIND OF A MAN WITH PTSD

JAMES KEITH

JAMES KEITH
AUTHOR

I'll Always Remember

SYNOPSIS

For nearly thirty years, James has kept his inner demons trapped in his own mind. One day, his mental health got the better of him and there was nothing he could do to hold the memories in anymore.

Being scared of the social stigma attached and what others would think of him if they knew his past, he struggled to express his feelings to anyone. Instead, James decided to write it all down and share his experiences with the world.

Because of the nightmares and flashbacks James has suffered from due to his post-traumatic stress disorder, he talks through each day in order to help him cope.

In this book, James lays all his struggles on the table: flashbacks, memories, self-harm, abuse both witnessed and received, alcohol addiction, loss, pain, suffering—all of his struggles are just a glimpse into the life of someone with severe mental health conditions. This story shows his progression through his illness. Follow his story so you may learn and understand what the highs and lows are like in the mind of someone who wants nothing more than to regain control of his life.

James puts his pen to paper and delves down deep, telling about his feelings of neglect, torture, lies, abandonment, and what it means to survive when he is left to fend for himself.

CONTENTS

I dedicate this book to my brothers Robert and Ricky, and my sister Sabrina. I would also like to thank my wife, Claire, for the support she always selflessly sent my way. My closest friends, Greg and Jade, without you guys, this book wouldn't have come to life.

I dedicate this to people who have struggled with abuse throughout their childhood, people who have suffered in silence, and those looking to find hope and closure in their lives.

If you are lost in your mind, if you are suffering from a mental health condition, if you are holding yourself from speaking because of the social stigma associated with mental health, my book is for you.

I was like you, too, and I have pushed through the odds of my life. I hope for this to reach out to you and help you, you who have suffered and are now trying to become the person you have always wanted to be, I hope you recover.

With hope and love,
James Keith.

PROLOGUE

In the palm of my hands, I could see my life laid out as if pieces of shattered hopes. When I couldn't sleep because of my worries, I only saw myself walking with the same person, every night, in all of my dreams. My name had lost its meaning until someone called me out until someone stared into my eyes and saw me for who I really was.

I waited for one person to offer their hand out to me, never realising I had to reach out to myself first. I had to memorise the movement of my hands to remember myself. I had to let my fingertips move freely with the flowing winds, open my heart for others to see, and now, I understand how I have come here pushing through every day.

Under the sunlit sky, I am with myself, searching for the better me, walking ahead with the wind. I am leaving behind the harrowing memories, the hurt, the unknown, I am now picturing the world as is, moving with my life in my hands only.

INTRODUCTION

My name's James Keith. I was born on the first day of January 1986, in London. For the longest time, I have dealt with a weakening mental illness; panic attacks, anxiety, and sleep disorders have gotten the best of me. I have yet to come across a day that will make me whole.

I started writing this book which I refer to as, "Start with Gratitude", it is a journal I write in daily for about five minutes; a journal that asks for my thoughts on gratitude and I would love to share them with you, my readers.

03.9.19 – BACK TO THE CRADLE

MY THOUGHTS

You tell yourself today is going to be a good day, a day you can look forward to. But, in your head, you tell yourself it isn't any different. You sit there on the highs of the see-saw; in the unknown, wishing for your weighing thoughts to disappear.

The hardest question is, where do I even start? If I may bring myself to begin with anything, I feel all alone in this world; it's as if no one has time for me. I mean, I understand people are busy, but being alone and being lonely are two different things. I spent my life helping, listening to others, but then again, my question is; what about me? Where is everyone when I need them? Why do I feel all alone? It often clicks in my mind no one would even notice if I didn't wake up one day; no one would care. I hate myself. Since I was a child, I always aspired to become a good person, to genuinely do good for others. Unfortunately, I always felt people avoided me because I was a smelly poor kid in the school. I hated going to school, I hated when people judged me and never spoke to me. I wondered what was wrong with me, I didn't know what I needed to fix. So, the best I could do for myself and others was to hide myself away from the world. I began isolating myself and it then transpired into my adulthood. I continued to isolate myself even when I hated the feeling of loneliness; like you're on your own. I tried my best to go back in the past and find some moments I could hold on to, but I only always saw myself looking at disappointments and despair.

I clearly remember my father. I remember everything. My mother was in the hospital as she had just gone through a hysterectomy. I was sitting in the dining room, at the table with Robert, we were having tea when Dad came in. He shouted at Robert; screaming it was his fault Mum was in the hospital because he does nothing to help. He then asked me to leave the room.

But I stood in the doorway. In that moment, I saw something that left in me a trauma. I could see something inside me change. I saw a change in my heart.

Dad became very fierce towards Robert. I saw him pushing the chair Robert was sitting on. I still remember his voice; crying and gasping.

"No Dad", he had said, but then Dad took his belt off and hit him. Robert was gasping, pleading Dad to stop, he was screaming in pain. Dad didn't stop. It was almost as if Robert meant nothing to him. He pushed Robert around the room, hitting him continuously as if he had forgotten to stop. It went on for about 15 minutes. It was pulling my heart out of my chest; seeing my older brother getting hit from an angry man who seemed hell-bent on hurting him. I wondered why Dad did this anyway; why did he feel the need to come in and hurt Robert this mercilessly? I cannot even begin to imagine what would have gone through Robert's mind later that night. He must have been terrified. It sent chills to my spine; seeing my dad lose himself. I wish there was a way to erase that memory. I often think about that incident and many more we faced. To me, it wasn't needed; Dad didn't have to bring such trauma to our lives. It was heartbreaking and brutal. I, to this date, hate my dad for what he has done to all of us. I can't fathom how he could be so ruthless and not think about his actions and the consequences they would bring. I never told Mum about this because I thought she already knew. But only recently, I had a word with Mum over coffee, and to my surprise, it was the first time she had ever heard of this.

"Why didn't you tell me?" she asked furiously.

"I thought you knew", I replied.

To this day, I can still hear the sound of the belt clashing against Robert's flesh; his screams for help. I want to forget. I want to brush this memory off of my head. The reality, however, is that it will stay within me until I stop breathing.

My relationship with Dad wasn't the same as Robert's. Dad was mentally abusive to me than he had been to anyone else. He would shout, abuse, and threaten to break my games and toys if I didn't do what I was told. It would happen when I would forget to give him a drink or if I were being too noisy. I was only a child, but it scared me because I knew he could get violent. I was always scared of being the next one for a beating. So, I used to do exactly how he would direct me, especially when he was angry. He was clever though, he made sure it never happened in front of Mum. As I grew, I was sure he knew what he was doing. I was sure he did that for fun, for his own personal satisfaction. It made him happy when he tortured others. He knew exactly what he was doing. But, his need for violence still did not make sense to me. I can't even recall my dad ever giving me a hug, probably because it never happened. I can't remember having any good moments with him. Honestly, he never played with me. He spent all of his time just lying on the sofa or out drinking if he wasn't at work.

I still remember how he argued every day. Every single argument brought something with it. I was always scared, scared enough to hide in my bedroom under my duvet; hoping and waiting for Mum and Dad to just stop shouting at each other. I didn't have the courage to come out of my room whenever they argued. Dad was so aggressive, and he would just threaten her if she tried to defend herself. I hid because I used to think if I'd come out, I'd be caught in the crossfire. I just didn't want Dad to hurt me.

Recently, I have had flashbacks of my dad; I will share them throughout my story.

SABRINA'S SCARS

Some wounds do not bleed, for the hearts bleed for them.

When Sabrina was just 11 years old; my mum was in the hospital. I lived in Norfolk then. Mum wasn't very well. She had two large Quincy's in her neck just before Christmas. Mum was supposed to take me to work that morning, to dock gate 20 in Southampton. When we got in the car, I figured something was seriously wrong, she couldn't speak and was clearly struggling to breathe. It was in that moment I realized how powerful the feeling of fear was. I knew I had to take her to the hospital urgently. I wanted to help my mother. I needed to make sure she was looked after. She is my mother, after all. I took Mum to the hospital where she was examined and was then admitted into the ward for emergency treatment. I was so terrified; I didn't know what was going to happen to Mum. I was afraid to lose her.

On a Sunday morning, dad told me I would have to take Sabrina to see Mum in the hospital. I had to take her on two different buses to get her to the hospital to see her. I didn't do this for Dad, I did this for the two of us because we were both on the verge of breaking. We loved her and didn't want to lose her. More so recently, I have come to know there were many more abusive incidents towards Sabrina. She told me Dad touched her inappropriately when Mum was in the hospital recovering. I am proud Sabrina finally spoke about it. She said she remembers everything clearly. It happened when she asked Dad if Mum was going to die, he told her to not overthink and get in bed with him. Being only a child, she didn't think it was inappropriate because she had slept with Mum a lot. It disgusts me to my core, but I have to let this out. Dad had asked her to come close for a cuddle and when she did, he started to touch her vagina. I had tears in my eyes when I heard this. I felt so angry, sick to my core.

It was our dad we were talking about. I wanted justice and retribution for his actions. I couldn't believe what I was hearing. How on earth was it okay for a father to inappropriately touch his 11-year-old daughter? It really disgusted me and makes me question the fact that he is my dad. He does not deserve to be our father; he wasn't ever deserving of it. Instead, he was always a vile predator who tried to satisfy his sadistic needs.

Mum started to recover well and had started eating food again. She was finally able to leave the hospital on December 24th, 2003. Sabrina and I were happy to see our mother healthy, especially the day before Christmas. I felt safe when I knew Mum was coming home. I had to take care and look after Sabrina while Mum was gone, and honestly, I wasn't quite prepared for it. I cooked her meals and I ensured she was taken and picked up from school. Dad didn't do anything he just left us to it and I guess, it was better that way.

Sabrina then told us about another incident that happened four years later, when she was only 15. She was changing in her bedroom when she saw Dad watching her. It scared her; made her feel extremely uncomfortable. She said it was so disgusting and creepy that it sent chills down her spine. Even worse, he continued to watch and told her not to stop. It disgusted her enough to make her run and lock herself in another room. She stayed in there for a long time. Sabrina always said it was the exact moment she realised she wasn't safe around Dad anymore and this was exactly when all the flashbacks resurfaced. The scars Sabrina received from these experiences must hurt a lot. I can imagine because she had to keep it in for so long.

Maybe in fear of the reprisal she could get from Dad if she spoke up about it. I feel disgusted because of him. I know now, for sure, he was a predator, and he fixated on my underage sister. Whatever he has done to my sister and my family, it makes me feel so violently sick. He must face consequences for what he has done. When we talk this out with Mum now, her face turns pale in shock; contemplating where she was when all of this was happening. Well, she was at work.

THE BOXING MATCHES

Man is given two roads to choose after a painful childhood, one is to keep the cycle going, the second is to become a person who puts an end to it; once and for all.

I recently had a conversation with my brother Ricky; it was our first conversation in 11 years. I had called him because I wanted to know if Dad had done anything to him too. I wasn't surprised, yet again, when he told me what he had been through. It turns out my dad used to force him and Robert for boxing matches, all for his own entertainment. They were forced to hit each other until the other one would be on the floor. And that whoever would lose, he would have to wear a nappy or be punished from David. The moment Ricky told me this, I understood how mentally sick my father was. What I can't fathom is how a father could force his own children to fight each other, that too, brutally. I mean, what kind of a satisfactory feeling can someone get out of it? I thought beating Robert was the lowest he could get, but I was yet to see more of his abusive traits. After what Robert told me, I was reminded of a conversation I had with my dad. He once mentioned his uncle Ian; he was a boxer, and he made Dad and his brother Dennis fight as kids. Was he re-enacting his own childhood? If he had been through the trauma and trouble, shouldn't he have stopped the cycle instead of reliving it? My mother wanted to know where she was when he would force Ricky for these boxing matches, everything came as a surprise to her. Ricky recalled Mum being out, drunk on vodka. It came off as a surprise to me, I didn't know Mum had issues with vodka, I was quite surprised when she told me otherwise.

I was as hurt and upset as Ricky continued, Dad hit him with belt buckles whenever he misbehaved. I was so sorry for he had to go through that, no one is deserving of anything of that sort, that too, from their parents. No child should ever have to go through that. And then, Mum told me how she found a note in Ricky's bedroom. It said,

"Mum is a cunt because she is with my dad", she was hurt, left to no choice but to call his biological father to take him because she didn't want him to hate her for the rest of his life.

When Ricky was young, he found 5 pence piece lying on the floor at home. Out of innocence, he took it to school, so he could buy Robert and himself some snacks. The two thought they could finally buy something of their choice to eat. But, when Ricky came back home, he was immediately asked where that money went. Ricky told him he took that 5 pence piece to school to buy some snacks and to his answer, Dad got very aggressive wherein he hit Ricky with a belt buckle across his back. Ricky can recall to this day, the touch of the metal buckle hitting his back, tearing his soul apart. I can't even begin to imagine how it must have felt. I could feel the hurt in the winds of his breath, how he hates Dad for treating everyone nothing less than objects, the hurt that echoes from within; he says he wants to erase memories of Dad. He wants him to leave and never return.

FUCK OFF FOREVER!

Words are more than just words, sometimes they are the waves that pass through your soul, leaving you with memories that hold you up high in the cloudy heavens, but sometimes, the same waves hold you from keeping your head above water.

And as time passed, Dad lost his ability to stop himself from drinking. His existence reeked of alcohol; it was as if his addiction knew no boundary; he pulled all-nighters drinking. And then in 1995, my aunt Lorraine came to live with us. At first, dad was nice to Lorraine. Lorraine is my mum's sister. Mum brought her home after she saw how her sister was living. She didn't want to see Aunt getting hurt and just couldn't leave her. She didn't know things at home were equally as bad, if not worse? Aunt had learning disabilities since she was six, she was overweight and relied on food to trickle down her stress. She would eat all the food, steal money and cigarettes regularly. My parents didn't want to let this stealing off the hook, they would shout at Lorraine. I remember Lorraine stealing a 5 pence coin from my money pot. It agitated Dad, he pinned her up against the wall and the sound of fear ringed from her eyes. I thought he was going to hit her, but he pushed her away and told her to

"fuck off forever". Why did it agitate him so much when he knew she wasn't in the state of knowing what was wrong? Why couldn't he understand she was a person with learning disabilities? He should have known better; he should never have scared Lorraine. I have yet to see him treat Lorraine like a normal person.

I had a transformers toy I really liked; it was one of my favourite toys and I never spent a day not playing with it. But now, the same toy brings with it a memory that threads through my soul. I remember walking into the living room and seeing Dad standing in front of the toy cabinet. I went in to look for my toy, but before I could reach for it, my dad picked it up from the sideboard screaming at me to not leave

"my fucking things lying around", and instead he threw it on the floor, breaking my favourite toy. I was only eight then, seeing my Dad break my heart and not just my toy, I could feel the rage and hurt instigating in me. I couldn't play with the only thing I held close to my heart. I ran straight into my bedroom, pulled the sheets up on me, and cried with my eyes ringing sounds of agony. What was in him that pushed him to do this? Had he known how much I loved that toy; would he have still done this? I wonder if things dear to us ever meant anything to him.

Why do we look at others and presume that the hurt they go through isn't as significant? Why do we fail to realise we are undeserving of hatred and misery?

WHY DAD?

Some questions will remain unanswered. And sometimes, it is better that way.

Back in the time when my mum was in the hospital, I and Robert's school uniforms were washed on a boil wash by my dad. I'm sure he knew how to use the washing machine; the machine only had a dial on it. It was unneeded to ruin our uniform with the heat of the boil wash. I guess he knew no stopping, he made us wear the same uniforms to school. It was awful and many made fun of me that day. I don't understand why he felt the need to do that? Besides, wasn't it obvious we would get bullied in school? Did he not care for the thing's others would say to us?

There was a time when we lived in a bungalow, this was before Sabrina was born, perhaps in 1990 or 1991. I was with Robert, we started to feel hungry around seven in the evening and asked Dad if we could have a sandwich. He was watching the TV, and we couldn't very well hear what he said, assuming he had agreed. Anyways, we were happy to have something to eat, went into the kitchen and opened the fridge, and to our surprise, Dad slammed the door shut screaming,

"I SAID NO". We couldn't stop shivering in that moment, thinking what had happened suddenly when he had said yes before. I remember going to bed sad and hungry that night.

MY MUM HATES CHRISTMAS

Occasions without the warmth of love are just reminders of a painful life.

Mum and Dad used to play darts. They started playing darts in Bitterness Park, which was only a 15-20 minute drive from home. They went out to the pub every evening. They would usually leave home at about 19:30 and return around 23:50. Mum was the one who used to drive because Dad never got a license. Dad would come home drunk, instigating an aggressive argument every night. It went on for several years. I never understood their need to go to the same place, meeting the same people every day. I went with them for a couple of times though.

Since Mum and Dad used to work almost all the time, Christmas wasn't an off for them either, which makes Christmas dinners an unneeded thing. I remember when I stopped getting a stocking. I was about 8 years old and was told that I was too old for it now; that really upset me. I remember Christmas' being lovely before things of these sorts started to happen. I remember the decorations all over the house and the efforts Mum always put in. But, as each year passed, the excitement trickled down, making Christmas just another day for us. I remember how Mum started saying she hated Christmas, maybe she used to say it because she had no other reasoning for it. The only Christmas dinner I can remember having as a family was when my uncle stayed over. We all sat around the table for a meal, my father began quivering and his eyes rolled to the back of his head. I had no idea what was going on,

Mum and Uncle took him upstairs. He came down a few hours later, said he was okay, and then started drinking whisky.

As Sabrina was growing up, she stopped spending time around Dad. I understand why she had stopped and I can't blame her for it, it's even surprising she is still trying to live in the same house as him. I cannot ever fathom getting used to living like that, seeing the same man live unapologetically, without the feeling of fear in his eyes. I do not think I have been born with that courage instilled in me. Sabrina is brave, unlike me.

Robert and I were trying to move on with our lives, but Dad, he had no stopping. Many times he screamed, threatened and said things of all sorts, all because our rooms were sometimes a mess. One day, when I was around 10 or 11, he grabbed Robert by his arm; dragging him out of my bedroom as if he was some object. He did it because our bedroom was a mess. He dragged him upstairs, pushed him down the stairs, and turned to tell me,

"I have been planning to take you to football and this is how you treat me?" Like always, my mum was out working. It flashes in front of my eyes and the sound of his screams quiver my body. I think Dad didn't realise he was the one mistreating us, but I still didn't want to hear that. I didn't care about football. I think he never realised the trauma he was drawing in the canvas of our heads. On cold, gloomy days, I sit back and think; had he known how much we hated the aura he had always poured on us? I sit for hours, but my questions remain unanswered.

Before Robert landed a job at Curry's and had a

second job as a postman, the abuse lessened, and eventually, Dad just stopped.

LEARNING IS EARNING

Learn, not just to become a better earner, learn to become a better man.

In the September of 1997, I started secondary school. I was extremely anxious for I didn't really have any friends. My school uniform was usually always dirty, not ironed, shoes worn out. I was bullied every single day at school for being smelly, ugly, and poor. I hated going to school. I hated getting bullied. I tried all sorts to get out of school. Before I could even blink, my time in school that was supposed to bring me warmth, turned south. I purposely messed my uniform many times, so I could skip school. I just had never the courage or strength to set my feet in school; I was a coward, someone who didn't try to fix anything. It was the first time I had felt I wanted to die; blur the pain once and for all. I had no one I could turn to, and I was too embarrassed to talk to my teachers. I remember trying to tell Dad, but it seemed he didn't see me as a human. He had said,

"Men stick up for themselves, men aren't weak to feel sad", but I hated it. I hated him for my life. I felt like I was being pulled into a trench that didn't have an end; I was being pulled every second. Whenever I went to school, my anxiety blared loud like a siren in my head, blurring the voice of the world. The fear and anxiety of getting bullied, my inability to talk, it was all leading me to ends unknown. From the time when I was 13 to the time I turned 19, social anxiety instigated in me and found a home in my head. It pushed me to isolate myself from even the warmth of the world.

Looking back in time, when I was fifteen, my dad got me a job in the kitchen with him for the weekends. I think it was disappointing of me to think I was going to experience something better. I remember my dad shouting at me whenever I made the slightest of mistakes and how he used to call me 'crap' and 'good for nothing'. It didn't just happen once, every now and then, he would shout, scapegoat, and blame me for things insignificant. I wonder if it was humanly possible for someone to be as torturous as my dad. I remember my dad telling me to straighten up and get better at work because I was embarrassing him, he didn't want to be humiliated. I think he gave me enough reasons to hate that job. I couldn't stand the way he was treating me, and so, I wrote my resignation and left it in the living room. I wanted him to see my resignation letter and know how torturous his attitude was towards me. I think he figured soon enough; I could see his behaviour starting to shift.

By the time I started college, I had built walls around my heart, it seemed to me life was now better lived within my head.

College was okay, I guess. I spent my time fairly well and did my A-Levels in Mathematics, Business Studies, Accounting, and Computing. I completed my first year at college and couldn't complete the second one. Honestly, I just wanted to get my own place and get out of that house. I longed for freedom. I wanted it to happen as soon as possible. When I was 18, I got a job as a caretaker in a nursing home, unfortunately, it didn't work out. I went on to work with my mum in mental health; working in mental health has since then transformed me into a different person. I met my first girlfriend online who was 19 years old. She had long, dark coloured hair, a slim figure, eyes that were blue, eyes that saw past me, and a smile that instigated the best of my versions. She had eyes that glistened like pearls and a smile that bloomed my world even on the gloomiest of days. She was an amazing girl, but we realised we were too different to grow together, and so, we decided to go our ways. I think it was for the best. Sometimes I feel I had let her down, but today, I know she is living the best of her times with her wife. I got in touch with her after a few months of our breakup. Even then, we were as good to each other as we had been before and decided to stay friends. We aren't as close as we used to be, but we still talk over time.

IT WAS LOVE, I THOUGHT

What is love for you? I look at love as if it is a lifelong process, a process of never giving up.

I met a woman after a few months of being single. She was tall, long blonde hair that brushed her cheeks, and pretty blue eyes that drew me close. She looked like she was interested in me too. I was love-sick too as I was just 19-years-old and this 27-year-old woman was showing signs of attraction to me. One day, we went into a restroom where she kissed me and left after giving me her phone number. The following day, she picked me up and took me to her house where we slept together. I could see the world changing for I couldn't believe an older woman had slept with me. I felt everything was going well and that I was finally wanted. Somebody actually wanted to be with me. She always told me she was single and so, we decided to date. She told me that she had been through IVF and wanted children, but this has never worked. I even offered to pay for the IVF at one point.

Our relationship was kind of different. She would come and pick me up in the evenings and take me to unusual places where she would ask me to lend her some money, which was usually between £15 and £25. She would then get out of the car and go speak to somebody, usually returning after a few minutes. After three weeks into the relationship, I proposed. I was smitten and convinced I was in love and that I was also loved. She told me she loved me every day and accepted the engagement ring. I maxed out a credit card just to purchase the ring. Yes, I was stupid. Things started to change with time. She always liked expensive gifts which I bought for her. She always said money didn't matter, but now, when I look back, it seems money was all that mattered to her. With that being said, I had to take out a consolidation loan to pay off the debt. But one day, she asked to borrow my bank card, which conveniently went missing, all my money was gone. I then had to use my credit cards and my debts spiralled out of control.

I was still convinced and believed it was love, and I was being loved. But soon enough, I came to terms with the reality. I stayed at her house over the weekends and a guy came over, she went to see him downstairs and was gone for a while. I went downstairs and to my surprise, I could see the shadow of them kissing. I went back upstairs as I was upset and I waited for her to come back. When she returned, she was smiling. I asked what had happened and instead of giving me an explanation, she flipped at me, began shouting and swearing. I think it wasn't enough for her that she threw my things out in the rain too, I was completely blank for a moment. I couldn't believe this was actually happening. I saw everything as if it were love. I had never imagined this happening to me, I broke down and cried. In a moment, she had come back and asked me to come in, she took me back and slept with me.

After this night, the relationship couldn't last long no matter how much we pushed it. I loaned her a mobile phone on a contract. We were on a night out when she left it unlocked on the table. I didn't mean to invade her privacy, but I just couldn't control it. I saw a message from a man, an intimidating message she had initiated. I couldn't believe she told me I was mentally deranged for checking her phone when I confronted her. I stood up and walked out of the club, she came after me. Since I was naive at that time, I went back to her friend's house. We ended up sleeping together.

I might have been blind, but my mum saw this coming. My mum never liked her and warned me tons of times, but I never listened. One day at work, Mum told me she saw my girlfriend meeting another guy after work. I didn't believe that, so I told my mum to

"fuck off". I know, I wish I could take these words back for they brought a lot of damage in our relationship, Mum didn't speak to me for a few days.

Moving on, the incidents of meeting strange people in

strange places kept growing. In the end, she and I split up, we had to. She had run up a massive phone bill on the phone I lent her. I called her one morning to talk, but the conversation worsened to the point she literally told me to harm myself. I took an overdose of tablets I was prescribed; they were antidepressants; fluoxetine and sleeping tablets temazepam. I took them all with 100 ibuprofens capsules. I had completely lost hope, I wanted to die. I was heartbroken. How could she tell me she was in love with me, but treat me as if I was invisible? How can she sleep at night knowing she had caused me so much pain? I guess, she never loved me. She only loved what she could get from me. I was young, naïve, and too infatuated to see the reality she had hid behind her eyes.

My mum called me about an hour after I overdosed, she asked me what and how many had I taken. I was slurring, I couldn't feel anything, and she rushed back home and called an ambulance. I was taken to the hospital and treated immediately. I was visited by the mental health team. I felt ashamed and embarrassed. After a few hours of questioning and being given saline, medications, and other treatments through IV, I was finally allowed to go home.

I attended work the following day. I was lost, I felt alone. I was really scared; it was the moment I started regretting my decision. The nurse in charge came to see me, she was really supportive. I was granted an annual leave and was told to rest. However, I returned to work after two weeks, and she was still working there. I had to see her every day and act normal. It was difficult at first, but time went by.

In 2006, I went to Florida to see my family for the

first time. I used the money I got back from a cancelled holiday to Sicily which I had first booked for me and her. When she found this out, she was angry and told me she would have still gone with me. I went to Florida and when I returned late January, I learned she had been suspended from work for taking money from service users. I was asked by the manager about this and for some unknown reason, even to this day, I defended her. Why did I do that? I don't know. She was dismissed from her role and I never saw or heard from her again. To this day, I am grateful that our relationship had ended soon. It was toxic and not good for me. She tried to add me on social media a few years later, but I was far from letting her in my life ever again. I still have memories of her in my mind, but I am happy to have left her.

BE A MAN!

Be a man, be emotional, be empathetic, be kind to the weak, be man enough to not prove it.

Going back in time, in 2003, my father wanted me to be more of a man and work more of a manly job. I got enrolled as an apprentice plant operator. It was not the job I had ever considered doing or had any interest in. I only did this because I wanted my dad to be proud of me. I wish I had said I wanted to work in care. Working for the construction industry had always and will always tire me out. I would never knock someone out for doing something they love. I knew and believed this industry wasn't going to bring the best of my version, or that it would fit my needs.

I worked at Petersfield for a month which was yet another awful experience for me. I was made to work in the compound. I remember the foreman telling me to 'get that skinny lad on making muck, let's put some meat on him'. I was forced to mix up the muck using the cement mixer and this was my work for most of the days. One day, in particular, I was asked to come to the river bed as they needed my support. I felt glad after a long time as I was really liking the idea that they needed my help. However, when I got there, I saw why they wanted me. I was extremely disappointed. It was a piss-take, and I was expected to climb on top of a 360 excavator and walk across the boom arm. The whole purpose was to repair a tree that had been damaged by the 360. I was handed a black bin bag and some tree repair spray. They took me to climb on top of the digger and walk across the boom arm. I did as I was told. Honestly, it was scary and very slippery up there, I remember hanging onto the tree and panicking as if my feet would sleep before me. Once the job was done, I came down and asked them why they needed me for this. The foreman's reply made my heart sink, he said, 'Well, nobody else would be stupid enough to go up there.'

There were other incidents as well. It was as if people were being paid to bully me. I remember being told by one of the ground workers to fill a barrel with diesel. I looked at this barrel and told the ground worker that it says water only on it. He said it didn't really matter and instead of asking questions, I should just fucking do my job; fill it with diesel that is. I didn't know any better and just did as I was told. Later that day, the foreman came over to me shouting,

"Can you not read, you fucking idiot" I replied,

"excuse me", he then told me it says water, and I am so fucking stupid I cannot see that. I told him I was only doing what I was told and nothing else. He then approached the ground worker who told him I was talking shit. I couldn't believe I had been set up. I really hated working on that project and I couldn't wait to leave for the National Construction College.

SUICIDE

Humans are often, just, unhuman. They fear the powerful and tear the weak apart.

In September 2003, I moved to the national construction college in Norfolk. I took the train to Norfolk, reached and settled into my room, as fast as the train moved. After a few hours, other students reached the dorm, they were a lot older. I was 17-years-old. When I saw people moving around me, I didn't think things would go well, they were loud, aggressive and didn't seem to care about the opinions of others. Pretty soon, everything about them became apparent. I was bullied, yet again, even in college. I was the puny, skinny boy, and so, I became an easy target. I was an outcast; picked on, pinned down, and pushed up against the walls by my throat. I even had rocks thrown at my windows at night. They would bang on my door. I hated that place. I wanted out. Two of the guys, especially, were horrible to me. They would call me names and chase me, push me and hold me down. I felt terrified. I am sure it was funny to them; my life. I remember them trying to run a car over me, I had to jump into a hedge for my own safety. I never felt safe there.

Once, I had almost gotten into an accident. I had forgotten to apply the break to the dumper and it rolled forward and hit the bucket of the JCB. The guys then decided to bully me by the name suicide. I hated it because I had always had suicidal thoughts in school. I called my dad one day, crying

"I want to come home". He wasn't even interested. I was too depressed to think straight and ended up drinking a bottle of vodka. Unfortunately, I ended up feeling as if my heart was stopping, it did actually. I was rescued and taken to the hospital right away. When I woke up, I had feelings I couldn't identify. I felt awful. I even wanted to die. I wanted to go home. I just wanted to breathe in the warm embrace of my mother.

The abuse and bullying didn't stop until I grew scared of leaving my room. I intentionally broke my arm one day, smashing it against a digger bucket, so I could get away from that hellhole. I had once been to the director to report the bullying. He reassured me to not quit because he will support me. He also brought in two men and warned them if he hears or see's anything or anyone upsetting me, he would get them fired.

But I was too emotionally drained to continue. I returned home for a few weeks and went to work with my dad in the kitchen again. When my arm healed fully and my cast was removed, I had to go back. I was still scared, but I didn't want to disappoint Dad, I wanted him to be proud of me. Before I came back to the dorm, someone else had already started living in my room. I went to the administration building, asked where my things were, and then found them in bin bags, it felt degrading as if I wasn't wanted. I couldn't fathom the fact someone could do this in my absence? I was given another room within a day. The guys were still the same; horrible and devious. I think I had reached my point as at then, the same moment when I was putting things back in my locker. I could feel the cold tears brushing my face, taking the air away from me. I didn't think anything worse could happen, but I was yet to see the extent they could go, they stripped me naked. I was awfully done; I only wanted to dig the ground and disappear within it. In the very moment, I wanted to disappear into thin air, never to return. I felt sick to my core. I ran to the director to tell him I was going home. I left that place and never looked back.

ROBERT LEFT

I have always been fearful of Dad. When I was 16 years old, I wanted to help Robert fix his bike in the garden. Before I could even go out, my dad shouted, "you're not going out".

"Why not? I am 16 now", I replied.

"I said no, you're not going out", he added, ordering me to "sit in the armchair" until he said so.

"I am 16 now, not a child to be spoken to like that", I said while trying to ignore him. And like always, his unwarranted anger flashed in front of my eyes. I had to sit on the chair like he had asked me to, but as soon as I did,

I was hit by a trigger from my childhood. I remembered when I once told Dad I like Christmas pudding, but he tried to convince me I didn't. I insisted that I really did, he then got me a big bowl of Christmas pudding, telling me to not leave the table until I finished it all.

It was a lot for me to eat. Five minutes into eating, he took it away, telling me how I didn't like it. I hated being told I didn't like something. It felt as if he was saving it all for him, or as if he didn't want to share. Was he just being sarcastic to me? He definitely knew I couldn't eat all of that alone, what was he thinking when he made me do that?

Robert was 4 years older than me. When I was 16, I was randomly using the PC and came across a file that had Robert's pictures; pictures of him being held intimately by a man in the woods. There were more photos of him with men. I regret calling my mum to see the pictures, she gasped as she saw them. I guess looking back, there were many signs of him acting unusual. Robert had started staying out over the weekends. He always said he was staying with a girl, used to pack his bag and walk towards the end and around the corner of the street, waiting to be picked up. It was kind of unusual for him to wait far from the house if it was really about a girl, why couldn't she pick him up from the house?

Robert was confronted right when we figured something was up. He came out to Mum and Dad. I remember Dad telling me he was disgusted and that he could have gotten the other man arrested if he knew better. Dad couldn't accept Roberts's sexuality. He was a racist, an alcoholic who hated men who weren't 'manly enough'. I could see fear ringing out of Robert's eyes before he disappeared into his room. I remember Dad going into his bedroom asking him to choose his sexuality or his family. Was Dad this hateful and heartless to ask such a thing to his own son? I feel Mum could have stopped Dad from forcing Robert to pick a side, but as always, we had to do what he wanted. Robert left soon after and I haven't seen him since March 2002. I couldn't see him leave emotionally destroyed, unaccepted, he was my brother and I wanted to keep him close. I have memorised his existence in every vein of my body, my heart wants to know if he is in safe hands. I know how my feelings of guilt weigh me down every day. Robert had kept it a secret, knowing full well he wouldn't be accepted in the family. I should've known better.

Why has my dad's pride always been a priority to him; something more valuable than his own kids. What was wrong with being gay? Had he been accepting of it; Robert would've been with me today.

MY MUM'S A SURVIVOR!

You believe you cannot take it until it is the only option left.

I remember our lives swirling in front of my eyes, I think it always only took seconds for my dad to scatter whatever we had built as a family. I can recall the day when Sabrina was still a young, vulnerable soul. Sitting downstairs with my dad, watching fishing programs and eating biscuits, we were talking about fishes. It all seemed too calm as if the breaths of wind were still. I went upstairs to go the toilet. An argument had started when I was still upstairs, out of nowhere. I could hear the front door slamming hard, breaking the glass. I remember my mum saying,

"I'm taking my daughter away from you", I went downstairs to see the house in complete mess, with things broken, biscuits on the floor, chairs tipped over, if I were to draw it, I can very clearly remember where each broken piece was; scattered pieces of our hearts.

Today, Mum shared with me the abuse and hatred Dad sent her way since the start of their relationship. She recalls one of the early days he hit and pushed her to the ground, he was drunk, she said. She told me how he hadn't just stopped there, he had hit her whilst on the ground. She was screaming when one of her flatmate friends came home to check up on her, luckily, she had brought her boyfriend to stop Dad. Dad then left.

A few weeks passed since Dad left, Robert had burnt his arm and had to be taken to the hospital. In the hospital, mum saw my aunt, my dad's sister. She knew if his sister was here, he would come too. The following day, he had come back home in a black taxi, mum had taken him back in without any questions. I wonder why she let him back in. She knew how terrible of a man he was, what was she thinking before risking it all? I could see the hurt in her eyes when I finally asked her, she had hidden from dad many times, but he had always found her. She had even been in refuge a couple of times, but he always found traces of her. Ever since we were kids, she wanted to take us away from the hands of our father, but he had always kept it from happening.

I have yet to meet someone who I'd want to be like, I don't want to take after him. I'm not made for the life he shares with himself. I hate what he has done. I hate how he has ruined my head, my mind, and my life. I don't want to feel suicidal. I don't want to be the way I am. I have so much more to pour out of my heart.

You see people who have suicidal thoughts as people who want to end their lives, nobody wants their life to end. They just want to put an end to the wrongs.

I started self-harming when I was in school. I slit open a pencil sharpener to use the blade to cut my arms.

Self-harm isn't what it looks like; it's sabotaging yourself until you can numb the pain out of your veins. The pain inside of you doesn't know its way out; you hurt yourself to give it a way out, feeling more of what's on the outside and less of what stays stuck inside. The emotional pain still remains, grows from within, but subsides for a while.

I didn't want to be bullied and I didn't want to see my dad drunk anymore. But I knew his actions weren't in my hands. I could do nothing about it.

Today, I took my mother to the blue planet aquarium. We walked around for an hour. It felt as if I was actually living in a moment with my mother and no one was on the face of this earth. We didn't do anything for the longest of times. We watched the fishes swirl their way up and above, living wholly in the water; free to move.

Nature has that power. It moves you, soothes the chaos building inside of you. It lets you breathe free; free and above.

I felt free and away from things I had always been

scared of. I moved on my toes, with the feelings of the water around me; nothing could hurt me. Before we went back home, Mum and I stopped for coffee. I could feel the warmth of coffee in the air, brushing my cheeks. Mum looked ethereal when I pictured her cheeks smiling with roses filled in them. Mum and I talked about things we didn't ever tell anyone. I saw the face of my dad in her eyes and I didn't like him yet again. I, too, told her things I had known since I was a kid. It felt as if it was the first time I had poured my heart out, wholly and willingly. Today, I could tell her everything I had gone through.

As a parent, your worst fear should be seeing your child go to bed crying without you knowing.

04.9.19 – I WANT THIS TO END!

How can you sleep knowing you'll wake up in the same place, in the same rut of hopelessness?

Tonight, I cannot sleep yet again. I can feel my dad's screams echoing in my head, Robert's cry for help, and my heart tossing in my body. I don't even feel tired. I don't think I feel anything at all. I have taken my medications; my stomach feels as if it is in my throat. I'm hoping for my medicines to settle my anxieties down. I can't sleep and I can't stay awake, I'm breathing thin air. My mind is blurred with the sight of my dad; confused and static. I posted on a social media app last night. It's an app for people with mental health conditions and I received some lovely comments. I couldn't believe the courage it took for me to post on the app. I even posted a picture of myself and my mum, something I'd never do. I very rarely post pictures of myself on social media even.

I want to stop these feelings of shame, embarrassment, and sickness. I want to be free from the misery that has held itself close to me. I feel like I'm trying to move forward, but I am held back by my own weaknesses. I'm still that scared little boy who is afraid that if he opens up, people will think less of him. I don't want people to suffer like I have. I want my family to reunite, with nothing but love and reverence. We haven't been together for 27 years. I love my mum and I despise everything my dad has done and continues to do to this day. He makes me feel agitated, sick, and hurt; he makes me want to die.

Yesterday, I tried to contact Robert. I left him a message on Facebook, but he never replied. Sabrina told my mum he had seen the messages and didn't quite feel good about it. He told Sabrina he was hurt by what I said years ago. I regret what I said, I was only a child; a child who knew nothing.

"I don't want to share a room with him because I don't know what he would do to me", I had said then. I was wronged into thinking it was okay to hate anyone who was not straight, and again, it was my dad who had wronged me. He had instilled in me to hate anyone who wasn't white, to not pay any heed to the views of people of colour. I requested Sabrina to apologise to Robert for me, but I never heard back from him. It has really upset me because I honestly thought now I would finally get to speak to my brother again. Dad always tried to shove his views on me, telling me to always stick up for myself, that men cannot be scared, afraid, or weak. Men had to be tough. I feel that all the pressure to be a strong, tough man and to impress my dad pushed me to lose my relationship with my brother. I really wish I hadn't listened to what he had said. I wish I was capable enough to take decisions in my childhood and make the decisions for myself that best suited me, not someone else.

My head is a mess. I feel fragile, alone, lost, and sick by the face of the earth. I want the pain to go, I want the happy James to finally be able to live his life. My father needs to be confronted. He needs to face the consequences of his actions. I want Mum to have her four children together for the first time in 27 years. I want justice, a life where all of us can live without the ties of my dad's behaviour. I want to be able to eat properly again. I want to sleep at night. I want my family reunited. I'm tired of all this. I'm scared for my nieces and nephews, my sister and her husband, and aunt Lorraine. My father will never see my daughter again. I don't want her to live around his dark aura. I want to help all the victims of his abuse and I want to help everyone living in that household to be free from the risks of reoccurring abuses.

Dad still continues to drink daily which makes me worry for their safety and mental well-being. I have never spoken about my past, not to anyone! I have always hidden behind a fake smile and confident demeanour. I couldn't talk, I was scared and afraid of the stigma. In my head, people would be ashamed of me, like dad always said *no one likes a weak man.* Men have to be tough. I have suffered in silence my whole life. I don't want to suffer anymore.

The support I have been receiving has been amazing! My mum, Claire, Jade, and Greg have all been so supportive. Leah-Jane doesn't know, though. She is too young and will not need to know about her grandfather until the time is right. I don't want Leah-Jane to struggle. I don't want her to feel the emotions I felt and I don't want her to be afraid of people at all. My saving grace is that Leah-Jane is over 230 miles away from her grandfather.

Today, Mum and I went to Middlewich to meet Jade over coffee. It took us longer than usual to get to the coffee shop because the roads weren't clear. To me, it felt therapeutic taking a walk together. We stayed there for about an hour, talking about things as we were brewed our coffees. Before we left, Jade invited me and Mum to join her for a walk. It had only just stopped raining. It had rained a lot before this day. I would prefer walks over anything; you can see swaths of flowers blooming under the sunlit sky, breaths of winds threading their way out of our hair. I was glad Jade wanted to take a walk. Time moved with the wind after the rain had held off, birds chirped everywhere. After we walked around the mere, we sat down to talk for a while. We walked back and forth before we reached home, and I was in awe; in awe of the aura the world had to offer me.

THE FLASHBACKS!

What is it that ignites hatred in someone, hatred that takes the soul away with the lightest of the winds?

My father never raised his hands on me, a part of me wishes he had. The emotional trauma that came with Robert's hurt was a lot for me to live with, I would've preferred getting hit. I knew how easier it was to heal from the physical pain caused by someone, because the emotional pain had brought me to the grounds. There was a time when Robert had gotten into trouble, Dad made him pull down his trousers and had then hit him with his belt. I remember Robert crying in pain. Dad had always threatened to do the same to me, yet he never did. I was scared and I hated Robert being scared and hurt.

How is it even humanly possible for someone to feel better doing things as such? Was there all to his existence, being abusive? It was as if he loved mistreating us like it was his purpose of existence.

For as long as I can remember, Dad regularly drank bottles and bottles of wine. To this day, it has continued. There was a time when I woke up, and he was lying naked, next to me on my bed. He must have drunk heavy that night, reeked of alcohol and looked absolutely disgusting. I was sharing my bedroom with my sister that time. I remember being scared, hating what I saw. I did not want to see his bits and I did not feel comfortable having him that close to me. I had to get out of the bed. I was feeling so disgusted. I got out of my bed and into the bed with my sister. I guess my sister's bed was where he had intended to sleep, but because of his state, he ended up sleeping on my bed. I was overthinking because of what Sabrina had said.

I am too close to giving up now, it feels really tiring to see things flash in front of my eyes. I remember him coming home drunk every night, agitated and ready to fight my mum. I hated the sound of his voice when he shouted at her. One night, he just didn't stop screaming at her; there holds no reason for all of the abuse he was giving her.

He had openly called her names, instigating hatred and hurt in her. She had had enough one day; grabbing a knife and running upstairs, she locked herself in the bathroom screaming,

"fuck off or I will stab myself." Dad didn't stay in front of the bathroom door for long. He eventually left and went downstairs. I and Robert both went to check up on her. We begged her to not hurt herself, and after a while, she came out of the bathroom. She looked very distressed and emotional. She claimed to have taken an entire packet of paracetamol, she then collapsed to the floor. Robert called for an ambulance. When she heard this she got up and ran out of the house. She was eventually taken to hospital where there were no signs of drugs in her system. The shouting stopped that day, but it doesn't really stop. I often wonder why Mum did this. Robert told me this story in much more detail. Still I will never understand her true actions on that day.

I try to find happiness. I try to feel I am accepted, but it feels so burdensome to feel lonely. I hate the person I have become. I hate having social anxiety and isolating myself from the face of the earth. Growing up, I only had Robert and when he left, I was left with nothing. I saw my confidence and self-esteem crushing in front of me always. To this day, I haven't fully recovered from these things. I put on a brave smile and hide behind this pretence, yet I'm always screaming in my head. I want someone I could pour my heart out to.

LOVE'S A CURSE

If I hadn't stumbled on my way, would I have been any different?

2006. I still worked in mental health. I met a woman who was 30 years old, she was attractive and outgoing, extremely caring. We were together for almost 2 years. She had two children; a boy and a girl. They were really lovable and our relationship was good. I was so happy. We spent many days of fun together and really loved being in each other's company. She helped me get onto an IVA and helped me mature as a man. I learned so much about myself with her. She showed me I could be treated right too, that I didn't have to fear anyone, and that not every relationship ends like my last one. If I were to tell more, I could end up with a book of things I am grateful for having received from her. She helped me to no ends. I really did love her a lot.

Towards the end of our relationship, we went on a holiday and while we were in a restaurant, one of her children said,

"You'd never become a part of our family". It apparently upset me and she heard it too. For the rest of the holiday, we spent most of our time being quiet. She was now distant from me and didn't get close to me. When we returned, she asked me to leave. I went back to my mum's house, I was hurt. I found out the following night she had met a man who she slept with. I felt so heartbroken and betrayed. I didn't speak to her for many months.

A few months passed, and she left her job in the mental health sector to work somewhere else. A few more months passed and I heard she had applied to come back to work in my unit. I was scared and didn't want to face her. I wrote my notice for termination as soon as I found out and handed it to my manager. The following day, my manager spoke to me. I was convinced I would disregard my notice. She came back to work.

We didn't speak at first, she was still with the man she had slept with the same day we split up. The first thing she told me was that the computer broke at home and all my pictures have been lost. I didn't know what to say. I just walked outside to smoke a cigarette.

After a while, she began to message me on social media. I would find her messages on my laptop telling me she missed me, loved me, and that she wanted me back. I replied her. I told her the same thing. I still missed her; I was still in love with her. A few days later, her partner called me, telling me to leave her alone.

He threatened to attack me. I told him I didn't want any trouble. A few days later, she messaged me again to apologise. Out of anger, I left her partner a message telling him to stop her from messaging me. Later that day, she sent me a few messages to tell me how I was a spiteful little bastard for turning back on her. We didn't speak again until they split up. She got in touch with me again, asking me to meet her in a park. I met her and before we parted ways again, I kissed her. She then got in touch after a few months. She picked me up, and we went to her friend's house and slept together. I immediately regretted it. It was the last time I saw her out of work until I left working in the mental health sector in 2010.

THE BIGGEST MISTAKE OF MY LIFE

I wanted to be a saviour, but I think I was not meant to be one.

In the mid of 2009, I went through yet another tragedy when I lost one of the patients I shared a close relationship with. He was watching TV when it suddenly exploded, spreading the fire on the third floor of the building. He was taken into the embrace of God that day. I remember being so close to him, I was one of the only few staff members who could get through to him, help him bath, get him to eat, I even got his confidence back in walking. He must've been so scared. He did not deserve to die this way. He was found on his wheelchair behind his door, badly burned. It saddened me to the core of my heart that I had to pour my heart out to our company's counsellor. It was unreal for me to believe he wasn't here with us. The fire department had examined that he had died from smoke inhalation long before the burns and it must have only taken a few minutes.

I feel August 2008 was possibly another time when I came face-to-face with the biggest mistake of my life. I was taking care of a patient with Down syndrome, we used to feed him via a PEG tube. It was a fairly chaotic morning, I and one of the agency staff members were the only ones to look after 14 men. One of our patients from another unit came over and over to ask for help. I was feeding my patient with the PEG machine and it just didn't stop beeping; indicating that the food wasn't passing through. The nurse in charge kept trying to get it to work, but it didn't budge for even a second. A few moments passed and it started working again, but stopped a while later. I managed to find the nurse in the occupational therapy room. She was with the manager. I asked her if I could change the feed bag instead if in case that was the issue, she agreed and I changed the feed bag and the pump started to run.

One of the other patients from a different unit then came to me to tell me he had swallowed an AA battery as he wanted a colostomy bag. I was instantly worried for the battery could instigate serious damage to his stomach. I was asked by the nurse to immediately take him to the hospital and when I returned, the patient I was taking care of was troubled. He couldn't properly breathe because the feed had passed through really fast. He had supposedly consumed half a days' worth of food in only 30 minutes. He was taken to the hospital and was treated right away, however sadly, he passed away from bronchial pneumonia nine days later. I was insanely guilty, felt broken, and destroyed and to this day, I blame myself for his death. Not a day goes by when I do not think of him and how his death was always because of my inattention. Why did I have to touch the bag? Why couldn't I just be patient and wait for his nurse? I often find myself asking these questions. It just hurts.

I blame myself for letting him and his family down. I feel horrible. A few weeks later, I was interviewed by the governing body for Health and Social Care. I was eventually suspended from my position for two days in December 2008. I remember this was scrutinised by the governing body as so much time had passed after the incident.

When I got the letter from court, I was summoned to the coroner's court. My mother was supportive, but father barely cared for our lives. I was cross-examined by the coroner and service users' families. It was an experience I'd hate to relive. Soon after, court declared that the situation was rather accidental than intentional, the coroner added that the way we reacted in that situation was excellent, we did everything we could to try and save his life. Still though, I think I am to blame myself for everything. To make matters worse, this case made it into the local newspapers where I was named and shamed. It was also posted in one of the national newspapers, but it wasn't detailed. It made things fairly difficult for me, many relatives of our patients called me out on this tragedy. I was scared of attending work. I really wanted to leave. I didn't want to work there anymore.

JADE HELPED!

I had a visitor one day, Jade, she came over to see how I was doing. She had come after meeting my mother and came over to have coffee with me. I felt safe talking to her. I really liked having my friends over, it made me feel a different type of a feeling. We got all of the reptiles out. First, we got the bearded dragon out who we call Beardie. I was absolutely amazed at how Beardie behaved with Jade, she behaved so calmly it was unreal. I haven't seen Beardie that relaxed before. After this, we got George, the tortoise, out. He was hiding in his shell, but he was obviously happy to be handled. We then went and had a look at Houdini. Houdini is a Leopard Gecko. She is called Houdini because she always used to try and escape when she was little. She would always be hiding behind the backing of her tank. Jade was amazed at how soft Houdini was to hold, and she really enjoyed handling Houdini. Houdini is very placid and loves being handled. Finally, we got Michael out. Michael is a chameleon. He has, what we like to call, mood swings. Michael initially did not want to come out of his tank, but in the end, he accepted. I handed him to Jade wherein he started pinching her and climbed all over her hands, he was a lovely shade of bright green, but a few minutes later, he went dark green again, so we popped him back in his tank. It was nice to see Jade after all this time, we could catch up on some TV and have tea, really. It felt relaxing.

05.9.19 – VIOLENCE IS NEVER THE ANSWER!

My emotional reservoir is filling slowly like an hourglass, like the sounds of the screaming and despairing reality is spilling the reservoir of my life.

I went to bed early last night, around 21:50. I was exhausted from working and wanted to sleep. I stayed in bed for about two hours before I managed to fall asleep. My nightmares came running again, as if Dad was coming home drunk, shouting and screaming at Mum. I was hiding in my room under my duvet, shaking and scared to death because I thought he was going to kill her. Before I could think of anything else, I woke up to a panic attack; my shaky and sweaty state was strangling me to death. I couldn't fall asleep back again. I was scared to, but a few hours later, I dozed off again only to see my father screaming in my face telling me to be a man.

I feel so sick this morning. I feel so scared inside, I hate these flashbacks taking over my life, the nightmares that pull me into a rut of dejection. I wish one night I can stop seeing things and not wake up feeling violently sick.

The following morning, Mum told me how a few months ago, she intended to mix Sabrina's amitriptyline and diazepam in Dad's food to get rid of him. In that moment, all I could think of was the time I had overdosed. I hate how anything minor can trigger memories in me that I want to erase. I couldn't help but ask Mum why had she thought of doing it, turns out, she was as done with him as I was. I told her it wasn't worth becoming a person like him, our actions can always turn back to us. One day, he will have to bend to his actions. She assured me she didn't really intend to do it, treating violence with violence is beneath her.

A part of my life revolved around arguments filling in the emotional reservoir of our lives. When I was 16, I had bought a baseball bat for safety. I did so because the spinoff of my dad's mood was frequent which sacred me. I was far from the extent my dad could go to after witnessing the abuse he had in him. Not long after I bought this, Dad became aggressive towards Mum. I picked up the bat. I wanted to use it so bad, but I didn't leave my room. I hid under my bed; I was scared to confront him. I allowed the abuse to continue. Could I have ever hurt my dad? I was not able to hurt anyone. I was not born for that life. It upsets me in my own mind when I see others struggling, but I cannot bring myself to hurt anyone. I feel guilty when I accidentally kill an insect. I don't like violence. I don't like fighting. I want to live in a world that is peaceful, one where everyone lives embracing the gift that is love and nature. In the world, this, sadly, isn't the reality.

Mum went out today on her own for three hours. She

told me she was going to have coffee to help herself from her thoughts. I honestly thought she had been gambling today as she very recently got her salary. Mum used to gamble a lot in her past when I was younger, especially on payday. I wasn't sure if Mum was telling me the truth. So, I trusted her when she said she was going to go to a coffee shop. She then told me she was going to tell Dad everything over a text. She told me that she had informed Sabrina of this. This, of course, made Sabrina panic, she had asked Mum not to do it as it does not feel safe. Sabrina was worried that if Dad knew that this has all come out and Mum wasn't there, he could potentially do some harm. Sabrina wanted to protect her children and I told Mum to take assistance from the law before taking any decisions on her own.

I could see fear ringing out of my mum's eyes, she said she was not able to face him all alone. She doesn't know what to do on Sunday. I, too, am not ready to confront my dad as yet. When I hear his name, though my heart rushes with rage, I still feel scared. I sit here and as I write how I feel, I reflect on myself. I feel weak, lost, and vulnerable. I feel like a burden to everyone. I want people to accept me for who I am. I don't want people to just pity me. I want people to like me, and for them to want to be around me. I've never really had that, not in my own mind anyway. I come with problems and I hide these. I get defensive. I get scared. I run away from confrontation, but can anyone blame me. Being told my whole life how I have to be a man has scattered the person I really was. People may see me as someone who can very conveniently, confidently lead the world ahead, but I am not it. I'm scared of being a failure, letting people down. I want to be okay, but I'm not okay. I'm hurt so bad inside.

The abuse continues to plague my mind and I cannot shake it off of me.

EVERYTHING'S A MESS

I should have understood who I really was, even when I saw myself in the mirror at my lowest, I should not have trusted how I saw myself in that moment.

The house I grew up in was always dirty, messy, and smelly. Doors were always damaged, carpets were always stained or removed, and the house always reeked of filthy smell. We never had money for repairs.

I remember seeing a school class photo that was taken in 1995, everyone was in uniform except me. The children told me I ruined the photo. But we never had the money to get ourselves new uniforms. Kitchen cupboards started to break and were never repaired. Even to this day, the kitchen cupboards have missing doors. No carpet, slippery stairs, and improper flooring, the house still has that terrible damp smell. Gardens were always a mess, overgrown, with bags of rubbish strewn down on the side of the house.

As a child, I was only allowed to take a bath once a week, on Sundays. I always remember Dad saying it was to save money. We never even had a proper boiler or enough hot water for one of us to take a bath. As a child, I don't ever remember owning a toothbrush. Dad never cared for personal hygiene, in any way. I can't recall him ever having a bath or even a wash, he would just stink of sweat or alcohol. My hair was always shaved. It seemed like a convenience to my parents; mum used to shave my and Robert's heads just like Dad's. I never had to go to a hairdresser until I started to earn. Everything was always to save money, never for the benefit of our family.

My teeth, to this day, are damaged because I had never the privilege to take care of myself. I am missing many teeth. Most of them were removed when I was young. I even continue to shave my head. I guess what I was used to getting done has transpired into my life as an adult, too.

The bathrooms were always disgusting and smelly, I hated that room so much. There was dirt and grime everywhere. Walls were dirty and clothes were always left about. The outhouse was particularly bad, full of dirty clothes in black bin bags always left there. When I think about this room, I can still smell it. I hate going back to that house and seeing the mess it is in and I can never recall Dad cleaning or helping to fix anything. I cannot even remember the last time my father cooked a meal; he would just be in the pub or lay on the sofa watching television.

It occurred to me that I hated how I looked, and why wouldn't I? Bullying and hatred at school, unappreciated at home, and anything that could bring me down to the ground happened to add up in my lack of self-esteem. I just wish I had more courage to be able to take more pride in how I looked. I'm a smelly, poor kid who wants to break free from the demons within me. I've tried nothing but to mature into a decent adult. I've tried to be everything that my dad is not. I want to be a good person.

I want to be someone who cares, someone supportive, a bigger person.

The young in me was suppressed, taken away from me, but the adult in me wants to put a rest to those emotions, wants to break free and become whole again.

Dad needs to get his comeuppance for the trauma he has put us through. I can't let him die as an alcoholic, not until he faces me and my family. He should be in prison, yet I'm still scared to take the actions for it. I hate shouting. I hate the fact that I know he will deny everything. I want him to suffer like I have suffered in my mind, all alone. I tried to make my own bedroom my safe place. I painted the walls, laid down a new carpet, bought a new wardrobe, and a new bed. I had a door fitted as well. I had previously used a curtain as a door which gave me no privacy or dignity. I had to decorate the room. I had to have my own sanctuary, a place where I could go for my peace of mind. I always kept my room clean. I cleaned it every single day. I didn't want my room to be like the rest of the house. This was my area, where I could sit, feel safe, and be away from the terrible smell and mess of the rest of the house.

The bedroom I used to share with Robert had a section where there used to be a door; it led straight into the kitchen. My bedroom was an old dining room which was converted, its old door was boarded up and plastered. In the summer, there were hundreds, if not thousands, of ants on this door. I and Robert would have to spray the door with an ant killer or tape it up using sellotape. Dad barely ever helped, he would just sit on the sofa, make me run errands for him. He could never be bothered for anything, all he tended to do was drink and watch sports.

I think Dad played football as a teen, or as a kid. He always pressured me into playing football like he did. I doubt if I was ever any good for something like it, I preferred reading and writing more.

After Dad continuously persisted, I joined the primary school team. I remember one particular match; I was brought on as a second-half substitute. I didn't know what I was supposed to do as they put me defence. Startled, I just stood on the line the entire time, I played awfully. After the game, agitated, Dad continued shouting at me, telling me I was useless for I had disappointed him yet again. I could see my confidence breaking down, despite all of what I had tried for him. I didn't play football again.

It is currently 21:20PM. I feel tired and I know I need to rest. I'm honestly scared to go to sleep. I don't want to have my nightmares flash in front of my eyes. I wonder if there's anything that can help me get some sleep tonight. I honestly do not know. If dad comes into my dreams tonight, I don't think I will ever sleep again.

THIS TIME, GREG HELPED!

If only you reach out to one person, you can save for yourself one regret.

Today, my friend Greg came over to see me and mum. Greg is an old friend of mine; someone I've known for about 10 years. He spoke to me of experiences that he has had in his past and how CBT has helped him overcome his problems. It was comforting to see Greg as I had not seen him in a year. We talked about video games, but I told him I haven't played them for about two years now. He then asked me to try and see how I feel about them again and try to get back into them. And so, I thought why not, I then brought down a console from upstairs. As we started playing, it was actually a lot of fun and I was glad to have my old friend play with me again.

After this, he showed me some board games he had brought over with him, and we played one. It was a role-playing game where you read a card, roll the dice, and then slay the monster. It was a team game, and we had to work together. Greg really likes board games. Spending time with Greg made me feel happy again. I hadn't seen him in such a long time and it was nice to see a friendly face once again. We spoke about seeing each other next week, and we decided I'd go and see him the next time.

07.9.19 – THE PILLS DON'T WORK

Is it the cold, gloomy night that is keeping me awake, or is it the harrowing experience of my childhood?

I went to bed at 10PM last night, I was so tired and exhausted. It was another horrible, restless night. All I could hear was endless shouting, drunk dad falling all over the place, threatening to smash everything in my room. I tried to change my thoughts, but subconsciously, I couldn't do this. I only got out of my bed to spend another night sleepless, it's been five long nights. I feel alone, abandoned, and I feel trapped in my own mind. I'm scared, I can't focus anymore, I'm weak, I'm worried I'm letting everyone down. I don't want to cause anyone any more pain. I don't want to be a burden. I'm so sorry for being insecure and weak.

I just want to be happy, I want everyone to be happy. I have taken my medications; I'm hoping maybe someday they will work. Someday, I will stop feeling so sick. Why, is an answer I want very desperately. Why does my life have to be so complicated? Is it the years of abuse? I have a lot of questions unanswered in my life. My brain is ticking over, trying its best to find closure somehow.

I went to Chester zoo with Mum, Claire, and Leah-Jane some days later. I was really looking forward to going and when we reached, it was a bit quiet, but then it started getting busier. I began to feel agoraphobic. I went into the Jaguar house only to turn around and leave as for the crowd that remained there. I felt my chest tightening after this, I became more aware of my surroundings. I didn't want anyone close to me, I wanted to escape. I felt anxious and I wanted to go home. I'm so scared of everything at the moment. It is driving me insane. I want to be able to be around some people, at least, if not many. Perhaps I can only see my social anxiety lingering in my head, blaring like a siren.

I have always struggled with crowded, busy places. I need to know where I can escape to. I need a safe place. I am so embarrassed and ashamed of myself, why am I like this? Could it be from being embarrassed at a busy party by Dad? I remember the Christmas party at work, he was drinking crazily. He got me and my mum a drink, and as he came over, he fell over and dropped the drinks all over Mum. He behaved terribly; grabbing people, and being very vocal. Very opinionated. Aggressively loud to other people attending the party. It was so unpleasant to see my father being controlled by alcohol; he honestly did not know what he was doing. After the party, we started walking home, Mum and I felt as if our blood was flowing with nothing but humiliation. Mum was angry and dad kept dropping behind. He was staggering all over the place and could not walk straight. As Mum and I continued to walk, we heard a loud bang, he had supposedly fallen into someone's car. He had smashed the headlamp with his head, I went back to help him get home. Mum left the two of us alone. I don't really blame her, part of me also wishes I should've left him on the road, that day. I don't think what was it in me that pulled me to help him. I couldn't leave him lying there.

The following day, Dad had a blurry memory, he had clearly forgotten the mess he had created, but I didn't. I remembered each second of the night. I had to go to work feeling very embarrassed, I really hated how he behaved. Even when he was told about his actions, he didn't just seem to care. It was rather funny to him, the hoax he had caused; unapologetically, he just continued to laugh on his behaviour. How could he think it was acceptable of him to laugh on his embarrassment? It baffles me and I guess I'll never know what was running through his head.

I have now decided to be open and honest with my feelings. I know now that I need to get better, I need to come to terms with my demons of the past. It sounds so easy, saying it. I have huge mountains to climb, but the mountains must be conquered. If I don't, my past and thoughts will all consume me and leave me in the darkness for the rest of my life. People are worried about me; I am worried about myself. I am neglecting myself, my existence. I am continuing to eat next to nothing, smoking a lot, and I need to make changes. I need to try and make myself feel good about myself. I don't want to keep hurting the people who care about me.

I cannot keep feeling so exhausted, fatigued, and broken. I need rest and a lot of it. I walked to the shop this evening. Claire was talking to me, told me she noticed something about a cardigan she got Leah-Jane which wasn't a part of her uniform. I did not like this and insisted that we use her proper uniform. This conversation triggered a flashback of going to school as a smelly kid. I remember being asked to take off my jumper in a drama. I did this and other children said,

"look at the state of that". My shirt was grey, not white, it was stained and dirty. I only had one shirt. I didn't have money to have more. The shirt I had was way too large for me and hung off me like a potato sack. I never took my jumper off again even when I was asked to. I had hardly any socks. I had to wear the same socks for a couple of days. They were so worn and had holes in the toes. They were so uncomfortable to wear. They would cause my toes to become very red and very sore.

My shoes were damaged and my feet always hurt. The soles would all be damaged, stones and water would always get into my shoes. I had verruca's and blisters regularly. My underwear would be soiled due to episodes of incontinence. I would have to wear these for many days, as I didn't own many pairs, perhaps maybe only two. I would often wear sports shorts as underwear to try and keep them clean. I hated sitting in my own filth. I've never told anyone about me soiling myself, allowing it to stay in the little underwear I had and sitting in it. I am so embarrassed, ashamed, and I am so scared of people knowing. People will think I'm a disgusting dirty bastard, but I wasn't. I was a scared teenage boy. I was embarrassed to buy underwear or ask for any help.

When I think back on those moments, I start to feel

sick. I cannot believe how I got used to living that way. Today, I wouldn't wear the same item of clothing for more than 1 day. I wash everything once I have worn it. I don't ever want to feel that vulnerable again. I wouldn't want anyone to go through that nightmare.

I had a small Sunday job when I was 12 to 13 working in a bakery with Mum and Dad. My job was to seal the sandwiches and then label them. It started fairly early around 6 am. I got paid £20 a week, plus £5 pocket money. I'd bank £20 a week and the £5 I could spend on what I like. I used to go out and buy lots of snacks. Dinner was always very basic and I don't recall eating lunch or breakfast on many occasions. If I did eat breakfast, it was usually a bowl of cereal. On so many occasions, we didn't have much food in the house. I hardly ever remember having a home-cooked meal, I was very skinny as a child, always very hungry and looking for something to eat. Home-cooked meals were always made using tin foods. There was no love or effort put into the meals. Both Mum and Dad just didn't seem interested in cooking for their children. It really did affect my childhood, was anyone ever interested to grow as a family? I eat very plain; I never make lunch and I very rarely eat breakfast. When I was a child, I only ate the snacks I would buy for myself. The £5 that I used would never go that far. My snacks would only last for a couple of days, I would then go back to being hungry. This is what I now do as an adult. I sit down and I pick and eat. I always make sure that Leah-Jane is fed well. I just pick at food. I guess it's from the old habit of just eating snacks and not knowing what a decent meal is like.

Today, I tried to boil two eggs for Leah-Jane. Such a simple task normally. I couldn't even manage this, I messed it up. I completely misjudged the timing and the eggs were still raw when I tried to peel them. My mum took over and continued to boil 2 more eggs for Leah-Jane. My mind is a mess, its mush. I hate this feeling of loneliness. I feel helpless. I don't want people to hate me, I just want to feel accepted, to be liked for who I am, not what I am and what has happened to me. Suicidal thoughts come into my head. I think if I'm not here I cannot feel anymore. But then, I cannot and will not hurt the people who I care about. It's so easy for me to think of the easy way out. However, my easy way out is a lifetime sentence to everyone else. It would crush all my friends, my family, and people who care about me.

My stomach hurts and so does my foot. My nails have got really long, and they are pressing my other toes. The easy answer is to just cut them. But, I can't. I wish I was able to just do such simple tasks and find the motivation to do them. It makes no difference, pain anyway, the physical pain is not masking the emotional pain. I don't know what to do anymore. I cry for help but I don't want to burden anyone. Am I fighting this alone?

I remember when the bullying got really bad at school. I was sitting in the food technology class and I heard a voice say,

"James Keith really stinks." Everyone joined in saying I looked dirty, ugly, smelled, and I was poor. I needed to be hosed down and scrubbed. I sat through the entire lesson with my head in my hands crying. I guess all the signs were there. I mean, look at me, damaged shoes, dirty, smelly uniforms, my breath must have been awful.

One teacher wrote a letter to my parents, asking them to attend parent's evening as they had concerns. I guess she was probably the only teacher who noticed there was something wrong. I got rid of this letter, though, my parents never saw this. Neither my mother or father attended a single parent's evening when I was in secondary school. I guess they never really cared about how I was getting on. Or cared about my education. I always wanted them both to show some interest in what I was learning. I had never any support or help with my homework from my parents. I was just left to it. Why? I remember sitting for my exams, longing to hear a 'good luck' from my parents.

I didn't like school at all; each day passed with me feeling as if torture was all that my life had to offer to me. No one noticed I was suffering. No one spoke to me or cared about what I was going through. Why did we never have any money to buy new clothes? It was pure fucking hell. I had no escape, a drunk at home, Mum at work, and bullying at school.

It is now 22:25PM. I feel tired of thinking about these things, yet I don't want to sleep. I can't bring myself to think what will consume me tonight.

08.9.19 – MUM'S STRUGGLING

When I close my eyes, I only see a struggling child looking for an escape, but when I open my eyes, I see everyone struggling to breathe.

Yet another night, nightmares and flashbacks swirling in my veins, and I think of giving up. It is hard for me to fight my thoughts and struggle every night. I'm beginning to wonder how it would feel to sleep now. Mum has just left, it is 08:00PM she now has a long drive home and my father isn't working today. I am thinking what could happen the moment she walks through the door, it is rather funny to know one of my dreams was of my mother, too.

In a dream, on Friday, she disappeared for three hours. She tells me she had been gambling, that she does it for an escape. Mum had always worked long hours, and on days she was off work, she would usually disappear for many hours. It was only as I grew older that I knew where she was going. She always went to Eastleigh; she had become addicted to slot machines. She would put all her wages into the machine, leaving herself with no money at all. I remember going with her and trying to stop her, but she wouldn't listen to me. I worried how their behaviour was going to pay for the expenses of our house. I always helped out Mum by lending her money. I even paid for her flights to America so she could attend her father's funeral, which was a difficult time. I was told by my aunt Donna about my granddad passing away, he had acquired pneumonia and sadly this was the last battle he was to face. I had to call my mum at work and give her this saddening news, it broke my heart to do it and I know it broke hers too. Mum went alone to America for her father's funeral. Dad didn't go because he hates America. He always said he would never step foot on it. My father sure hated Americans, I haven't been able to know why. I only wonder why wouldn't he support my mum. It was about her dad, he needed to stick by her side at least. But I think his pride was always only of value to him. I absolutely despised this.

Dad was extremely selfish, only ever did what he wanted to do. He would never listen to anyone's perspective or opinions. There could only be one way, and it was his way. If one had ever wanted to voice their opinion out to him, he was always only critical of it and not just constructive criticism, but he would try and make you feel bad. Make you feel like your views were stupid and irrelevant. He loves others being in control of him, he absolutely loves having power over others.

I also had dreams about my birthdays, I honestly cannot remember the last time I even got a birthday card from my parents, let alone a birthday present. My mum says happy birthday to me on social media, she doesn't even call me. My father has not said happy birthday to me for as long as I can remember. I never remember any birthday celebrations. Dad always said, 'men don't do cards, these are for women and sissies.' Birthdays were always very lonely, being at home, Mum and Dad being out at work. I would sit there in my bedroom on my birthday and I would just feel empty and alone. Why would parents disregard their kid's birthdays? For 27 years, I've kept these things in my heart, with no one to pour my heart out to. Now, I can talk. I can slowly let go.

It is now 09:15, I am exhausted, tired, my eyes are barely open, yet I don't want to sleep. I don't want my nightmares to get the better of me.

Later that day, under the shiny sun, I have to take Leah-Jane to her swimming lesson, but I do not feel like leaving the house. I want to lock myself away. I can't even watch Formula One anymore. I'm losing interest in all the things that I used to love. Mum has gone, and I wonder when will I see her again? I don't know. It saddens me that she would only visit me in Manchester after 5 years due to my poor health. Funnily enough, the last time Mum visited me in Manchester was due to poor health when I was hospitalised in 2014, with community-acquired pneumonia. I take it Mum only wants to put the effort into visiting me when I am not well. I don't know how to feel about that. I have always made the effort to drive down to Mum to see her and my family. Why couldn't the same effort work both ways?

So, I took Leah-Jane swimming today. Claire went in with her as I was sitting in the waiting room. Flashbacks and memories came back into my head. I was once in a swimming PE lesson in school. I knew swimming was coming, so I tried so hard to boil wash my underwear, so when I got changed no one would notice the stains of urine. I was so anxious about this that I washed them multiple times using a lot of detergent and stain remover. But it didn't work, the stains were still there and I had no choice but to borrow some of Robert's. I was so incontinent at this stage I didn't even know it was happening to me. I tried so hard to conceal them, but one person saw them and told everyone how

"I was Keith, a smelly boy who shits himself." It was awful, horrible. I didn't know where to hide my face, I couldn't run out of the school at that very moment. I had to attend the lesson and get into the pool even though I knew I couldn't swim well. I walked around the pool and jumped into the deep end to drown myself. To my surprise, a guy pulled me out of the pool. I didn't want them to save me. I didn't want their pity, and so I lied I fell into the pool. It has stayed only with me until today.

I wonder how the students didn't get tired of bullying me during the PE lessons. I often wore my full PE uniform under my uniform, so I wouldn't have to get undressed. But I'd just start to feel hot in the summers. There were no cubicles in the boys changing room and I tried so hard to isolate myself. I would take myself off into the far corners to keep away from everyone. Boys tried to drag me into the showers, would come up to me, and spray extreme amount of deodorant all over me; in my face, my eyes, my body. I only got rashes on my arms and armpits as this continued. I tried everything I could to get out of PE, but it was something Dad wanted me to do because he always said real men play sports. School absolutely messed up my mind. In the later years of school, I stopped my PE lessons. I had an in-growing toenail that kept me from taking any PE lessons, I was waiting for a surgery to have the nail removed.

After swimming, we went to a shop to get some chicken. I felt hungry for the first time in days and asked if we could get some breakfast. I was happy to have my appetite back because I ate well that day, but instead, I came home feeling sick.

As I think of my birthdays again, I can see myself wanting a birthday cake as a child. How come I was never given a birthday cake? I believe it is the only thing a child waits for the whole year. Now, as an adult, I do volunteer work on my birthday to blur out the memories I have of my past. Was it because my birthday is so close to Christmas? I don't know. Was I neglected, or is it all my own fault for not asking for help? I could never ask my dad, because to him, birthdays were for girls only. Mum was never home. Was I a bad child? Did my family hate me? I hate what has happened and I hate what still happens in my mind.

I took Leah-Jane to a local fair the following day in our town. Leah-Jane was so excited about the rides. When I reached there, my heart started racing because of the crowd. I felt sick and panic started to settle in. I felt like I couldn't breathe. I looked around and saw swarms of people all around me. I started to tingle. I didn't know what to do. Leah-Jane stood with me, telling me how she was excited. I wanted to get out, but Leah-Jane wanted to stay. I tried to get away from the crowd, but I couldn't. There were just too many of them. I felt dizzy and still feel dizzy now. I couldn't let Leah-Jane down, but now I'm on a knifes edge. I'm struggling today so much.

I have recently spoke to my mum to see if she was okay. She told me when she got home, Dad was outside. She told Dad I had PTSD. He asked what that was, and she told him it was post-traumatic stress disorder. He said he didn't know how he could be responsible for anything as he hasn't seen me in a long time. Mum said it's from the trauma from long ago. She mentioned making Ricky and Robert box for his entertainment. Throwing Robert down the stairs. Sexually touching Sabrina. Threatening to break all my toys. His response was

"I am going to the pub." He was in denial; he acted like a coward as he denied the trauma he had caused upon us. He never went to the pub anyway, but his response was,

"Well, if James is that bad, why he has not been locked up?" He isn't denying or confessing anything. I want him to confess and face up to what he has done. I don't want an apology from him. I want him to face the consequences of his actions.

Today again, I made a stupid mistake as I did when I was boiling eggs. In the shop I was filling a teapot, I was watching it but I overfilled water everywhere. I never make silly mistakes like this. Tomorrow, I go back to the doctors. Although I'm very nervous I'm going to still open up and tell them how I'm feeling about my lack of sleep. I've been smoking far too much and I can now feel this on my chest. I'm not ready to quit smoking. It numbs the pain in me. I really hope what I am doing here will help others in situations like mine. I feel there needs to be more awareness especially on mental health disorders. Many times men commit suicide because of the societal label

"Men are not weak", which stigmatizes the idea that men do not need counselling.

I keep spacing out trying to fight the flashbacks that appear right before my eyes, but it's not such an easy task. Things are difficult and I'm beginning to learn there is not much I can do, other than try and learn to accept them. But, as long as Dad is still in that house, I'll never be able to move on or accept it.

I would be biased if I said my mother had no role to play in all of the trauma. She should have noticed the signs; how could she turn a blind eye to what was happening in the house? She should have noticed I didn't have a clean uniform, that I didn't have much of clothing, and that I was coming home from school feeling worn out and tired. She should also have noticed that we weren't being fed, not properly anyway. I remember the last few months of living in that house. Every single evening, we were only fed baked potatoes and cheese. She should've noticed how underweight and skinny I had gotten.

It is now 21:10, quite late. Unlike other nights, I do not feel tired. I guess it's because I don't want to go to sleep. I don't want to see everything replay in my head. I don't want to feel scared. I'm hoping tomorrow will be a good day. I'm hoping that I will be able to relax. In that moment, I messaged Sabrina to ask how Mum was doing, she told me Mum was struggling, but she'd be fine. I asked

Sabrina to watch over Mum before she settles in. As for Dad, I know he is around, hiding in his bedroom.

Recovery lies within something. I guess we all need to find our own way. There will be a way, it's not going to be easy, but I'm going to try my best to find it.

09.9.19 – I DIDN'T PLAN FOR THIS!

Sometimes, living is hard as is, your body doesn't even move with a heavy breath of wind. You stand still.

Tonight, I woke up again with a feeling of fear and anxiety in my own thoughts. I've become very jumpy in my sleep. I dream and feel emotions of pain and suffering, I see visions of being shouted at and threatened. Right now, I have to take Leah-Jane to school. When I return, I will tell more of my story.

Today, I am all alone. Mum has gone home, Claire is at work, Leah-Jane is at school. No one in the house but me. I feel really alone. I feel really scared of myself, but this is something that I'm going to have to face. I can't run away from my own self. I may start to feel I've been abandoned again and that people don't really want anything to do with me, but I will have to push past my thoughts. It is hard not to feel like I'm more of a convenience and only wanted when I can be useful, given what I have gone through. When I'm not wanted, I feel discarded. I feel people don't care anymore, it sure is a horrible feeling. But it is still something I have had my entire life and something that will never just change overnight. I feel these feelings are a depiction of my past relationships, where I was neglected after I fulfilled their motives. As I sit here alone, I am wondering how things would go at the doctor's today and how will I go on with the day until I pick Leah-Jane from school at 16:00. I'm worried today is going to be a long day. I don't want to keep trying to get in touch with people because it upsets me when I don't get anywhere. The easier option is to let people come to me if they want to talk to me, but I feel that may never happen.

IT'S GOOD TO SEE YOU HAPPY, MICHELLE!

It is better to go back in time, at times, what may seem insignificant can take you forward in life.

I had a childhood friend called Michelle. She lived next door to when we lived in Bursledon. We were like two peas in a pod, did everything together and had an amazing friendship. I can recall our time together. We used to play all day and as much as we could. Mum was good friends with Michelle's mum, they used to talk together. Michelle's mum was a midwife, and she helped Mum when she was to give birth to Sabrina. I don't ever remember Mum being pregnant. I just remember that I woke up and I remember seeing Mum's tummy so huge. I knew I had a baby sister. Michelle and I stayed friends for a long time before we had to leave Bursledon, there were new developments in progress. We moved to Hedge End.

I still continued to see Michelle as she moved to Thornhill, but only for a short while. Mum lost contact with Michelle's mum and then I lost contact with Michelle. This was 1995. I was only young, and only until 2008 I was able to find Michelle again through social media. I met up with her in Southampton, it feels nice to know your childhood friend has now a family of her alone. I, though, am still alone. I have nothing. Not much to show about my life except the scars I will never speak of. I was so happy for her, but in my head, I could only ask why I was so deprived of happiness.

MY PHYSICAL SCARS

I think I know, now, it is not the irremovable scars, but the struggle that's keeping me together.

I have physical scars. One of which is on my right arm, just above my elbow that looks like the letter J. I was six years old, running around the living room when we lived in the house in Bursledon, I slipped and cut my arm on the doorframe and managed to catch my arm on a nail that was sticking out. I remember it hurting, going to Dad to tell him I had hurt my arm. He told me it was only a scratch, but it wasn't just a scratch. I knew I had hurt myself quite badly. I went to Mum to tell her Dad had said it was a scratch. I remember Mum shouting,

"it isn't just a scratch". She took me to the hospital where I had seven stitches in my arm. I will never forget that time because I think that's the first time, I realised that my Dad never really cared that I may have hurt myself.

Before this happened, as a young child, something was wrong with me that my parents hid from me. It was not known to me what my condition was or why was I frequently taken to the hospital. I remember one day my dad had to carry me to the doctors. He told me I couldn't walk for some reasons I do not know. I was examined and every part of my body was checked. I remember then being taken to the hospital where I stayed quiet for a few days. I don't think anyone wanted me to be aware of my situation. I really want to know why I spent those days in the hospital. I'm confused as to what went on. Why am I thinking what was actually wrong with me? Why couldn't I ask years ago? My mum was here all week long, but why couldn't I ask her?

11:00AM, my appointment with the doctor was scheduled, but was then delayed. When I finally went into the room, I spoke to the doctor. I told her about my sleep paralysis and uneasiness, how I had been feeling low. I told her about my childhood abuse, everything about my dad. I told her I had an appointment fixed on the 26th of September with a counsellor and how desperate I was to get better. She told me she had already a word with the team after my appointment on Monday last week. And that social services have already been contacted. When I heard social services, I panicked thinking they were going to take Leah-Jane away from me, but she assured it was to only help support my family. It still doesn't mean that I don't have concerns. I am really worried they are going to try and take Leah-Jane away from me and or if they'd think I am not a good father anymore. I called Claire, she told me it was just the early intervention team and I had nothing to worry about. She said this is just to see how we can support each other to make things easier for each other. I spoke to Jade as well, she also asked me not to worry and that everything was going to be okay, that Leah-Jane is well looked after and that I shouldn't worry much about it.

LET IT OUT, TALK.

Talk, talk when it's as overwhelming as the wind in the fall nights; talk if it tickles your heart, talk if it pushes you off the edge of the ten-floor building.

I once spoke to my mum, but she didn't seem to understand. Instead, she told me I would have to talk to my dad directly at some point. I told her I was going to speak to him when the time will be right, right now, it isn't the best time for any of us. I was also told I needed to contact Ricky, but I was yet to find the right time for that. I don't think I am ready as yet; my mental state doesn't have the capacity right now. I walked home, sat down on the sofa, and tried to gather my thoughts. I am hoping for everything to be okay. I have never once thought of harming anyone and I would never want to put anyone through anything.

I sit here now and worry that I have messed up and ruined everything. I absolutely love my daughter from the bottom of my heart. I would never want anyone to take her away from me. She is well looked after and I will do anything to make sure she is happy. She doesn't know how I feel. She doesn't know what's running through my mind, and she doesn't need to yet.

She is far too young to understand the complexities of my mental health. I want to get better again. I have great support from family and friends who have been absolutely amazing to me through the darkest of my days. I'm starting to feel a bit better and relaxed.

It has been a good day because I had been able to reflect on myself. I understand now that I need time for things to get better and there is a way out of these situations. I no longer wish to take my life, instead, I want to live my life. I want to be happy and free from everything in my past and I will do this. I will conquer everything with the support from people around me. I want my story to inspire others, help others, and encourage people to talk it It was hard for me to speak up in over 27 years, but please, don't be like me. Please talk about your problems, the right people will understand.

MAYBE I'LL GET SOME SLEEP TONIGHT...

Slow down, hold your heart in your palm and movc slowly, in your own control, in your own world.

I have yet to live a more positive day than today. It was therapeutic to relax and get past the thoughts in my head. I called Jade this afternoon, she was on her way to see someone. She told me she was in the area, wanting to eat something. I took this opportunity to see if I could spend some time with a friend. I felt more confident in my skin. I asked Jade to come over to the local fast food restaurant in my area. Jade came looking so happy, telling me how nice it was to see me. We ate and talked for a while. I can't begin to tell how happy I was to have someone around me after a long time. When I got home, Claire gave me a book titled

"Beat Your Depression." I was glad, it made me realize how people around me want to help with my recovery. I will read through, and hopefully find helpful tips that will help me on my journey. Claire is doing so much to support me and I really cannot thank her enough. Tonight, I am going to try to have a normal, easy night. We are going to watch a movie together for a long time. I'm beginning to relax again. Hopefully, tonight I will be able to sleep well. I don't want the horrible sleep paralysis to blur out, so I can rest well.

Before I went to sleep, I took a long, warm bath. It is the first time I took a bath in this whole week. I just wasn't able to bring myself to do it before. It helped me feel better, the warm, soothing splash of water running through my fingertips, calming the chaos within my body.

19:40PM right now, in the lounge, I am waiting to watch the movie. I cannot even remember the last time I thought about watching a movie with someone.

It really has started to feel as if tonight is going to offer me the best of this world. I feel I will rest well; I am looking forward to getting my peace back. The chaos within me, however, had come back rushing in my mind throughout the day, but I will write about that tomorrow. Right now, in this very moment, I will enjoy the rest of my night. I am going to relax, unwind, and enjoy a movie with coffee brewing hot in my cup.

10.9.19 – SOME THINGS JUST CAN'T BE FIXED

"I CANNOT TREAT YOU EQUALLY", WE REASON WHEN we lack acceptance.

When I thought I was going to rest well last night, I didn't know what awaited me. Last night, again, I had flashbacks blurring my dreams, scaring me for the memories I hold. I woke up feeling sweaty because of a panic attack; it wasn't even that hot. I woke up to a rather cloudy, windy day; one that looks like my mind, blurry and restless.

Last night I had a dream take me back to one of my childhood days, it must have been around the year 1989. I was 3 years old, I guess. We lived in a semi-detached house, I cannot remember the exact location, it may have been Chandlers Ford or Eastleigh. The back garden of the house had a gate that latched on to a wide alleyway. I remember Robert and Ricky being there. I remember they took me over to a guy's house where we played with his toys. I remember a toy called connectible; toy cars that can be interchanged and have their middles, front, and ends swapped over with other toys. I remember playing there for a short while and then going home. I remember Mum and Dad being very angry about this and shouting at me and my brothers for going out. I remember them saying that I was too young to be out.

In the same memory, I can remember Ricky telling me and Robert to go to the shop with him. We left from the back gate and went down the alleyway to a small shop to get a bag of sweets. But I remember Dad being very angry, shouting at Ricky, calling him a thief. I remember him shouting at them to not take me anywhere, to stay away from me. I then remember he hit Ricky across the back of his legs very hard. It was horrible to see. Why was he hitting Ricky and Robert and not me? Is it because they were not his children? I honestly think Dad couldn't bring himself to hit me as I was his son.

The only other memory I have of living in that house was when I went to a playgroup. I remember Mum taking me in and leaving me there. I didn't know any of the children there and this was the first time I can ever recall being around other children who were not my brothers. I remember trying to go into a play house. There was this girl, she was a lot bigger than me and I remember she wouldn't let me in to play because I looked funny for I was bald. It's funny how I can remember this. Perhaps it is because it was the very first time I was ridiculed for looking different. Bad memories stick in your mind for a lifetime. There really is no escape from them.

FRIENDS – THE ROPE I HOLD ON TO!

I was thinking a lot yesterday. I wrote about my childhood friend Michelle. We were so close, always played together, and when we both moved away, we still stayed in contact for a while. I used to love going to Michelle's house. I was so happy, and we played so many fun games. We would always sit together and watch the land before time on VHS. This was definitely our film. Michelle was the first girl I had ever kissed. We were playing upstairs in her bedroom. We were both very young and were sitting under the bunk of her bed. She had a friend over too, and she dared us to kiss each other. I and Michelle giggled and looked at each other and said okay! We then gave each other a peck on the lips. Because we were so young, we pretended to be grossed out and wiped our lips in disgust. It was rather funny. We were only just children. They always say you never forget your fist kiss. I won't ever forget that moment, it may have not been a meaningful first kiss. But it was still the first time I had kissed a girl and would be the last time I kissed a girl for many years.

Today, I am looking forward to meeting Jade, she is a very special friend to me and I have known her for 2 years. I work very closely with Jade, and we spend a lot of our time working shifts together. We have both been extremely supportive of one another throughout this time. We are both struggling to stay above the noises in our head, and are understandable and empathetic towards each other. I am sure we are going to meet up for a good therapeutic session today. She's actually going on holiday tomorrow, to

Tenerife. I am really excited for her as it's her first holiday since she was 16 years old.

She was in a long-term relationship with someone she had known for a very long time. The relationship had gone south right after, she started to show signs of discomfort and hurt. I remember her coming for work looking very upset and tearful. She told me so many times she had to leave the relationship, but she didn't know how. I sat with Jade for many hours, listening to her story and how she was scared to go home each day. It was fine until one day she told me she couldn't take it anymore. I asked Jade where her partner was. She told me he was at work. I asked her what she was going to do and Jade told me she was going to leave. Jade managed to finally get the courage to leave, and she has not looked back ever since. Jade is now a much happier person and much more confident within herself. She always thanks me for helping her and tells me she will always be grateful for all the support I had sent her way. Jade had the courage in her all along. All she needed to do was believe in herself. I am so proud of Jade and how far she has come. She deserves her happiness and I know she will now be happy and free to live her life the way she wishes, without any fear of upsetting anyone or causing any issues. Jade is very inspiring and has been really helpful to me throughout the last week. We have an incredible friendship, one that I cherish and will cherish for the rest of my life.

Jade has visited me today. When she came over, she read part of my story. It was nice to be able to share my story with a friend. She couldn't believe what I had been through and how I have managed to keep it under wraps for so long. After this, we had a nice hot drink and made a bacon, egg and cheese sandwich. It was nice to feel normal again with a friend around. Jade created a timetable for me, so I just didn't sit around all week doing nothing. It had ideas of things I could do while she is on her holidays to Tenerife. I am going to stick to this and send Jade pictures to show her that I have really been doing them. Jade also set up music on my tablet and has helped download some playlists for me to listen to as I begin to write my story. I look forward to the next week now. I have purpose and things to keep me occupied.

After we had breakfast, we sat down and watched a movie. It was lovely to be able to do normal things. Jade has now gone and I will miss her company over the next week. I have told Jade I want her to have a fantastic time on her holidays, and she deserves to be happy. I have told her to go and have the time of her life. She knows I will be fine. This is her time to enjoy herself and I have support here from Claire, Leah-Jane, Greg, and others. I look forward to picking up Leah-Jane from school and Claire coming home, so we can try and have a relaxing evening.

My Mum messaged me this morning to ask if I was doing well. I told her I was fine. She told me how Dad walked straight past her and ignored her as if she was not there. I am tired of having to ask Mum why she hasn't left him, why is he still there? She just says she doesn't know, that she cannot face this alone. I don't like the pressure of being forced into speaking to my dad. I will do this when I am ready. If I do it now, things won't go in my favour. Everything has to be reported correctly. I need to gather my thoughts, then when the time will be right, I'll do what's right.

Claire continues to check up on me to see if I am fine. Claire cares so much for me and I can see this by the look on her face. Yesterday, I picked up Leah-Jane a little later in the day. I got home. Claire was worried and had gone out looking for me. I did tell her I was fine, but because she knew how I normally feel, she got worried. I don't blame her for this. I would be worried too. I met up with Claire outside a local shop, and we walked home. I don't want my mental health affecting people who care for me. I want everyone to be okay. I want happiness for people I love and care about.

DOWN CAME THE LIAR!

I did it to fit in, I reason. Should I have to conceal who I really was, or should I have accepted myself first?

I think of many times in my life when I had lied about myself or my family. Why did I do this, one may ask? I think I did it to always make my life look better. For the longest time, I tried to conceal my reality to please people. I was always scared thinking if people found the reality of my life, they'd think of me as a lesser being, or simply just, pity me. At least that is what I thought in my head.

But today, Jade convinced me how I was worth it and that people should like me for who I am, and not the lies I tell at times. I am not proud of concealing my real self just so people would like me. It wasn't right of me to impress people, my intentions were wrong, which alone makes it wrong. I realise that now. It can lead to false friendships and I don't want people as such. I want friends who would care about me.

Right now, at this very moment, I don't feel like a failure for I have realised and achieved things beyond my control. As I move forward each day, I will write about one of my achievements in my life. Beyond my control, there are many successful anecdotes to tell, I just need to think more about the positive aspects of life.

THERE'S STILL A LOT OF FIGHT LEFT IN ME!

Find for yourself a new journey, if you don't, you'll end up in the same rut of despair and hopelessness.

July 2013, today is one of the days I want a purpose, a challenge to push me ahead. I wanted to do something that would urge me to invest my inner and physical strength. I spoke to some colleagues at work, we decided to complete the national three peaks challenge. We had to climb up the 3 highest peaks in England, Scotland, and Wales; Scafell Pike (978m), Snowdon (1,085m), and Ben Nevis (1,345m). We had to complete this challenge in 24 hours, including our commute time. We left on a Saturday morning. We had the 330-mile drive up to Scotland to first start from Ben Nevis, the plan was to leave at 07:30 and to arrive at Ben Nevis at 16:00, so we could try and complete the peaks in daylight. Our journey began, and we made the long road trip to Scotland, stopping for lunch along the way. When we reached Ben Nevis, it was raining and the winds were very strong. We had no idea of the feat we were about to undertake. So, we started our ascent on the mountain path. It was down pouring, and we were all soaked within a matter of minutes. I remember walking past a large rock and catching it with my stick, it fell onto my ankle.

I was hurt, but I was not going to give up. We were completing this walk for charity, to help raise money for a sensory garden. As we got further up the mountain, it became much less busy, and we began to start losing light. The rain and mist were intense and visibility was poor. We passed the waterfall and I thought to myself how further could this possibly be. Ben Nevis does not have a steep gradient, instead, it has a very long slow gradual gradient that just appears to go on forever. We progressed forward, cold and soaked. As we went higher and higher, I noticed a thick white area. I thought it was a cloud, but it was thick snow. I then realised I must be very close to the top now. I ploughed on through the snow and made it to the top of the mountain. It was amazing and was the highest point I had walked up in my life. I felt a great sense of achievement. I stood at the top of the mountain, raised my arms in the air, and screamed

"YES".

As I was coming down the mountain, I slipped and fell in the snow, my ankle had now swollen up. It took us only a few short hours to get back down to the car park, where we set off to Scafell Pike to complete our challenge.

The journey from Scotland to the Lake District took us forever when we arrived at Scafell Pike, the sun was shining, sky blue and it looked beautiful with Wasdale Head in view. We unpacked our equipment and got ready for the next challenge. I remember walking up this steep hill and when we got to the top there were stairs, so many stairs that needed to be taken. This was a lot steeper than Ben Nevis, but it didn't feel that far, you could see the summit almost immediately. As I reached the top of the stairs, I noticed a flat terrain with two options; one was straight directly over an enormous boulder field, the other was to walk the long way around. Because it was a race, I didn't want to take any chances, and so I walked towards the boulder route straight across. It was intense, physically exhausting.

When I reached the end, it was just a short walk up a hill and round to the top of Scafell Pike. We had now conquered the second mountain. As we started to walk down, a huge mist out of nowhere came from the sky. It was moving fast. I remember we joked about how we can race with the mist, down to the bottom. We did this and managed to get back down fairly quickly. We got back to the car and headed off to Snowdonia for the last challenge to take on.

The journey to Snowdonia was good. The roads were quiet, and we made great progress. Things were going well and we were on course to complete the challenge. However, we made it to Snowdon a little too late and had run out of time on the 24th hour. We decided to try and complete Snowdon anyway only to realise I had lost my boot. I must've lost it at Scafell Pike, unfortunately, we all decided to call it a day and come back.

We left Snowdonia but still felt as if we conquered the challenge. We planned to come back to Snowdon in a few weeks to complete the challenge. After a few weeks had passed, we arranged to visit Snowdon. I drove us down. It was very early in the morning, cold August morning, and I was only wearing a vest top, but it didn't stop me. We got ready, and we scaled the mountain very quickly, which was, by far the easiest mountain in the challenge. I realise how I loved trekking, outdoor challenges. We may not have done it in 24 hours, but we have climbed the highest mountains in England, Wales, and Scotland, that alone to me, is an achievement in itself. We managed to raise over £2,000 in the challenge alone. I was satisfied to have played a great part in a cause.

For the year 2020, I can't help but feel excited about the Manchester marathon I have signed up for. Claire and I will both take on the 26.2 miles of a gruelling run, something we have never done before. I don't think I have given myself enough time to get in shape for this. It is a bit late to turn back now. I have considered contacting personal trainers to help get me in shape for the challenge ahead. I am doing this marathon for a men's mental health charity. I want more men who have suffered like myself and others who have suffered for different reasons to be able to talk openly about their problems. I hate this social stigma, the perception that men are strong all alone. I am not my father, and I am much more open to talking to people. I will always give everyone my undivided attention if they wish to talk about their issues. I want to help inspire other men, to talk and be open and remember how there is always a way out if you just try to help yourself. It might feel as if your light has dimmed, but letting it burn down to nothing remains in your control. Take your action and control the way this universe works for you.

MAX- A LOVING MEMORY

I picked up Leah-Jane from school, she looks very happy and bubbly this evening, waiting to eat her brownies and seeing her friends there. On my way home from school, I saw a dog, a golden retriever who looked exactly like a dog I had, Max. Max was my childhood pet. Mum and Dad took me to the kennels with them to get a dog when I was 11 years old. It was in 1997. We looked at many different breeds of dogs that day. Mum took a liking to the golden retrievers. There were 3 of them, 2 females and a male. All 3 were barking and looked happy. Mum chose Max. When Max was taken out of the kennel, the other 2 dogs stopped barking and looked very sad, laying down on the floor and did not move. I can still see their faces to this day. Why do I think about these dogs? Maybe I was worried that they were all a family? I don't know. I just hope that they managed to find a good loving home.

Max was an amazing dog I grew up with, he was my friend for such a long time. I used to take Max to the parks where he would run around and enjoy being outdoors. Max was well-behaved and had a keen taste for polo mints. Max used to take his time coming down the stairs. Claire would get out the polo mints and Max would move so fast to get one. Max was still in good health when I left my Mum's house to move to Manchester with Claire in 2010. What has upset me was the fact that I was never informed of Max's passing. Max died sometime in early 2011. However, I was not told that he was poorly, sick, or that he was put down 3 months after. I was so angry at Mum for this and I asked her why didn't she tell me?

Mum told me that it broke her heart having to have Max put down, and she just didn't want to talk about it.

I did have other dogs; Buster, Mo, and Jake. I will talk about them tomorrow. Today has been so good and relaxing and I would like to continue focus on being relaxed, content, and feeling happier in myself. I do still struggle, and I am hoping that I manage to sleep tonight. I hope to feel better in myself and get a good sleep. After a positive day, I am sure that tonight may be the night where I sleep through.

Mum messaged me again this evening as I had messaged her earlier, telling her how I don't think Dad is going to talk. Mum replied with

"he won't unless confronted or even asked why." I then told my mum to confront him. She told me that it needs to come from the victims. I thought to myself, why couldn't she confront him? She was a victim herself. I told her to confront him, she told how Dad had only said 'yes' when she told him how she had spent 37 years of abuse with him. She thinks we will never get the answers we want from Dad.

Mum keeps asking me to contact Ricky and tell him I'm not coming. This conversation began to trigger me, but Claire intervened on my behalf saying I'm not ready for any of this. What I need to focus on is my own self.

I have spoken to Greg over the phone this evening. I am going to visit him on Thursday and spend the day with him, his daughter, and his dog. I really am looking forward to this. I have also walked down to Claire's parents this evening. It was nice to get out the house and go for a walk. I have had an evening filled with joy.

11.9.19 – THE GOOD TIMES!

AMIDST THE MANY THINGS THAT I DO, THERE IS always something that continuously fills the reservoir of my life with more and more hurt.

Again, I was hoping to sleep last night. I thought it will be it now that I was slowly getting better. I figured I was wrong when I woke up at times during the night, sweating and shaking with anxiety and fear, mind consumed by the experiences of my life. I cannot shake the image out of my head, the image of my father assaulting my brother violently. It's always in there, in my mind. I have already spoken about this, but it stays with me. I just cannot seem to get rid of it. I wonder why on earth I still hear the screams, the hits, smacks, even after 24 years. I guess it is hard to blur our memories. Even to this day, all the time, I say I can feel everything as if it had happened only yesterday.

Today, I have to take my car to a mechanic, for a quote on some damage on the front passenger-side. I am usually a very careful driver, a pinpoint driver, someone who can manage to get through any gap. But, a couple of weeks ago, I completely misjudged it trying to turn into a parking bay, I caught the front-end of the car. It was the day before I ended up in hospital because of my anxiety attack, I guess it was a warning sign of what was to come. It was a 17-mile drive to the mechanic, I am obviously worried about the cost, but at the end of the day, it is just a car. I have learned to accept that materialistic possessions have very little meaning to me anymore, what really matters to me is, life and people.

I took the car to the accident body repair shop in Trafford Park, I felt anxious as I did not know what the outcome of the quote would be. I didn't have to wait long to be seen. The gentleman came out and looked at the damage, he managed to repair the bumper and side panel and popped them back into place completely free of charge. It eased down my anxiety. All that was left was a quote for the re-spray as the paint had completely scraped off from the front bumper. After about 10 minutes, I was given a quote which I thought was extremely reasonable, which really made me feel better. I was only out for approximately one hour and 10 minutes; it was nice to get out the house again and to have some positive news instead of worrying for a very expensive bill.

I came home and I began to reflect upon my feelings. I remember yesterday talking about my pet Max. I also had three other dogs Jake, Buster, and Mo, and now I will talk about these three. Buster was a cross-breed between a Staffordshire bull terrier and a black Labrador, Buster and I were very close. He was sometimes aggressive to other people. He used to sometimes bolt out the gate if Lorraine ever left it open. Buster was protective of me; he was my best friend at the time and I loved him so much.

We got Buster in the year 2000. Sabrina would've been 8-9 years old. I remember she started to get louder towards myself and Buster did not take this. Buster ended up scratching Sabrina quite badly down her legs, causing them to bleed. It was this very day my mum was done with it. She said she didn't have a choice than to let Buster go in 2002. It broke my heart to see my best friend put to sleep. When I look back, Buster wasn't a bad dog, he just wanted to look out for me.

We got Jake in 2001, he was a German shepherd. We got him as a puppy, he was absolutely adorable. I remember he grew very fast. Jake was a gentle giant; he wasn't aggressive at all. He would play with Max and Buster; he was friendly towards me and my family. As Jake grew older, at the age of six, he became quite frail; his fur started to come off, and he kept losing weight no matter how much we fed him. We took him to the vets where they tried him on a treatment plan for eight months. This was to try and see if they could help him. During this time, one of our neighbours reported Jake to the RSPCA thinking he was a neglected dog.

However, Jake was undergoing treatments for multiple cancers. In the end, he lost his battle and there was no way for him to survive, so unfortunately, we had to have Jake put down. It was heartbreaking. I do miss my dogs, I miss them a lot, and they were a security blanket I could cuddle up with whenever I felt scared.

Mo, she was a beautiful black Labrador. She was amazing in every sense of the word. Mo came to us in around 2008. She was bubbly and very energetic. I remember her getting stuck under my bed as she was playing hide-and-seek with me. She loved going for really long walks with me and Max. I miss Mo. Mum gave her away in the end as we just didn't have the time to walk Mo as much as she wanted to. It was such a shame as I loved my dogs and still do, even though, none of them are here anymore.

I think back to myself and say

"why are there no photographs of me as a child" I always wonder. Excluding the one picture I have seen of me in a class photograph recently. There are no pictures of me as a child. I don't have any at all. The oldest pictures I have of myself are from 2006. My mum did take pictures of me as a child. I remember a camera, yellow in colour, every picture that was taken would have a holographic image of Hulk Hogan in it. This is because when I was young, I used to love watching wrestling. I remember Mum taking photos of me with this camera at the park in Hedge End. I remember seeing photo albums of me on my 1st birthday, but yet they have all disappeared. I guess it's because the house that I used to live in with my family is a shit hole, a mess, and everything is broken. Perhaps they were thrown out, I do not know.

Did my parents not care for the photos they took of me as a child? Shouldn't they be cherishing them? I guess, in a way, it is better, not having bits of those memories. I wish for many memories to brush off of my mind. Yet, I know for a fact they won't just go. I know they will continue to hurt me until I stop myself. It's not just the photos I don't have anymore, some of my belongings I know nothing of anymore, except the wallet. It is the oldest thing my father got me when I was 12 years old. A wallet I use to this day. I have had it for 21 years, but I no longer want to keep this memory of my dad.

I have talked to Claire and Jade about this, Jade has asked if she can buy me a new wallet. Another thing I have is the signet ring my father got me on my 19th birthday. It's a horrible heavy ring. I used to wear it until I was about 24 years old and it lies in a jewellery box since then. I accidentally saw his ring yesterday, looking at it, I felt sick. I have now decided to take it to a jeweller on Saturday to sell if off. I don't wish to keep anything that holds memories of my father. I want to rid myself of everything to feel clean, to restart my life. In the process of my recovery, I don't want anything of my past.

Today, it was difficult to run to school, when I reached to pick up Leah-Jane, I was not greeted. Instead, I was asked why I was so early. Why do we have to go now? Leah-Jane told me she wanted to play, that there was nothing to do at home and it is very boring. She then ran across the playground and hid behind a storage container. One of the staff members went to collect Leah-Jane whilst I went and got her bag. When I came back out to see Leah-Jane, she was walking towards me with a staff member. I don't know why she came up to me to tell me how I was a bad dad, how she wanted a dad better than me. It shattered my heart to hear the sound of her voice. For a moment, I forgot I could talk. She's only 9 years old, she is my daughter who I love unconditionally. I couldn't understand what made her say those words to me; they touched every vein of my body. I told her what she said was upsetting, hurtful, and how she's supposed to say such things. She apologised immediately and told me she loved me.

A moment later, she told me she had not a drink all day, she was really thirsty because she doesn't like water in the bottle I gave her. I felt awful as if I was failing Leah-Jane at this point.

If I bring myself to talk about one of my achievements again, I'll tell you how I overcame one of my fears – fear of heights. We go back to the year 2008 when I was 22 years old, I wanted to travel and see the world. After the relationships I had in the past, I wanted some time for myself, to do what I want to do. I thought the world was my oyster. So, I went to travel agents and booked myself a luxury trip to New York City all by myself. It was an August holiday and my flight was early in the morning.

I woke up late, panicking, I thought I was going to miss my flight. I lived in Hedge End and my flight was leaving from Heathrow. I managed to drive up to Heathrow in time. Even though I took a wrong turn I rushed through the check-in and security and managed to make it to my gate with 15 minutes before the flight. Now, the realisation had to slowly settle in. I had once flown on a plane before alone to Florida. But I was meeting people there. This time, it was my first time flying alone and going somewhere alone. I dressed myself up in a suit. I was staying in a very luxurious hotel. I wanted to feel special, not poor. I wanted people to notice me.

The plane landed in New York early morning. I managed to get a ride quite easily from the front of the airport to go to Manhattan Island where I was staying. I got to the hotel and checked in, and left immediately after. The first thing I wanted to do was get over my fear of heights. I head straight to the Empire State Building. I got there, the queue was short, and I paid for myself to go up to the outdoor observatory. When I got to the top my heart froze, I couldn't go outside. I could feel myself getting tense and very anxious. But I managed to fight this and pushed myself to go outside. I looked across at the landscape around me and took some photographs. I then looked down and my vision started to blur. I was terrified, but I had to face my fear. I managed to do this and I did this alone. I conquered a fear that had been in my mind as far back as I could remember. I went back down to the bottom after about an hour and went straight to the restaurant to treat myself.

It was the moment I realised I don't have to be scared of things anymore if I just push myself to better myself. I can face anything if I put my mind to it. I think, unfortunately, with time this feeling of empowerment dwindles away. It was such a moment and I just wish I have that courage again to face my fears. I was so proud of myself that I returned the following night and paid to go right on the very top observatory on the 102nd floor. I don't know if I will be able to get past my fears again, but we have yet to see the potential I hold within myself.

It's 21:00PM as I write this, Claire is taking a bath, Leah-Jane is watching videos on her tablet. I think about things others are doing right now, is someone dancing on her toes? Is someone brewing a cup of coffee? Someone is somewhere doing something like I am.. Jade is on her holiday in Tenerife, she should be arriving shortly. Greg is probably playing video games.

I know every person in my life is up to something this very moment. I care for my family and friends, I know that they care for me, too.

Mum, however, didn't mention Dad even once to me today. I think I am fairly thankful for that. I don't think I was ready for the pressure today. It occurs to me I need more patience than ever to be able to talk to my dad. I am hoping to sleep tonight. It would be nice because I don't see myself free for even a second tomorrow. I am going to see Greg and his daughter. I haven't seen Greg's daughter and it will be amazing to see her for the first time. I have something to look forward to tomorrow.

I have downloaded a meditation and mindfulness app, anyway. It's an incredible app and I have paid for the annual subscription. I am amazed at the amount of content on this app. I have done my meditation for today and I will continue with this daily. It was a bit difficult to keep my focus for the first time, my mind wandered. I found it hard to be at peace with myself for more than a minute. I am hoping for this to be of help. I am hoping it can make me feel relaxed and help me sleep. While I am happier than I have ever been, I have to yet feel more in my life.

It takes a long time for the scars to heal once the memories come back, once you speak out.

IT TAKES TIME

I cannot know who was hurt the most, I cannot understand the neglect we had to put up with. Does it not occur to people that they will have to come face off with their own wrongs one day?

I have a memory I often think of, an argument I can very closely feel. Dad was drunk and Mum was sat downstairs. Dad came down in just his underpants and socks. He began shouting at mum very aggressively for about an hour. I heard Mum saying,

"I need to go," before she left the house and sat in her car. She must have locked herself in the car. I remember looking out the window to see Dad in his underpants and socks, standing at the side of the car, shouting. A neighbour shouted out their window telling Dad to shut up. It only just agitated Dad more, I remember him telling them to

"fuck off". Dad eventually came back in the house and went to bed. Mum followed Dad a little while later. Why did Mum put up with so much abuse? Was I neglected due to my mum feeling mentally abused? Or did my mum just oversee what was actually happening to me? I have to ask both of them these questions, but I am waiting to be in a mentally strong position.

In my mind, many times, I have tried to forgive my father. I have tried to get along with him in my adulthood. I have even been on two holidays with him, to Mexico and Cuba. I will talk about these holidays another day, but I just wonder was I trying this hard to get past the hurt he had given me. Why did I need to put in all of the effort?

My father never calls or texts me. I have text him in the past, called him, never to receive an answer from him. He knows what he has done, yet he chooses to stay silent. It's his choice, but one day, he will have to face up to what he has done. I just hope for that one day. I just hope for my life to move on away from the past and my life to look forward to the future.

I think there comes a time in everyone's life where they have to understand that their actions may affect others. In many situations, it is harmless, knowing and accepting the wrong you have done. There are actions that bring consequences as disastrous as ever, in the long term. Shouting at someone in front of children. Someone raising their hand on someone else. It can happen anywhere, not only in our houses. What we must understand is that we're all needy of support. At this time, in this position, I need support, and I am getting amazing support from all the people who care about me.

In the last 10 minutes, I have been hit with an overwhelming feeling of sadness. Right now, it is 21:50AM, deep down in my stomach, I feel empty and sick. What has triggered this? Is it my depression hitting me hard before I try and settle down for the night? I am confused.

Claire was not being difficult today; she was just trying to get jobs done. What has triggered my depression now when I have been feeling happier? I guess it's an answer I won't get and one that will only add into my sadness if I kept questioning myself. I try to tell myself sadness is just a human emotion, but really, it's much more than that. It consumes me most days and I wanted to go to sleep on a high.

I want to apologise to everyone who I let down. My emotions are seriously beginning to get the better of me and I really don't want to feel this way tonight, or any night. Living with mental health issues really is a challenge. One minute you feel on top of the world and the next minute, you're having flashbacks and you want the whole world to swallow you whole so you can escape those thoughts.

I guess you could say it's like having two people in your mind, one who is rational, listens and understands and the other one who is screaming and being tortured. I try to focus on the rock that I have.

"One day at a time". Right now though I'm looking at each minute at a time. Trying to gather many thoughts, trying to control my mind. Trying to win the battle. Every day is a battle. It's a long and gruelling battle. Some days I win the battles and other days I lose. But I cannot lose the war. I need to fight. I need to find my inner strength. I need to believe in myself. I need to believe I am going to be okay. Right now, I am not okay. Right now, my mind is clouded. I write my story and my thoughts to help me process what I am thinking and I hope for my own story to help me understand who I am and not what I am.

Today, I made another silly mistake. For the second time in 7 days, I forgot Leah-Jane's school bag. I had to go back home and get it. I realised it before we got to the school and I turned the car around to get her bag. Why am I making such small mistakes all the time? Is it because my mind cannot focus? I guess I don't know. Should Leah-

Jane, a 9 years old child, take more responsibility for her school bag? Maybe she should. I have discussed this with Claire and Leah-Jane tonight. From now, we are going to do a check every morning before we leave the house to be sure Leah-Jane has everything she needs for school.

12.9.19 – SOME NIGHTS, IT'S WORSE

I SPREAD MY ARMS AROUND TO PROTECT THE NEXT person, will someone else ever feel the same for me?

Last night was awful, perhaps one of the worst nights I have had in a very long time. Waking so many times crying, sweating, and shaking. It has now been 9 days. I am beginning to struggle physically. I really do not feel well, I feel extremely cold on the inside yet the outside of my body is boiling hot. My eyes are stinging. My arms and legs keep trembling from time to time. I feel incredibly weak, as if I may just blackout at any time. I am really starting to worry about myself. I am beginning to feel isolated again. Maybe this is just in my mind, I don't know. My dreams were intense. I was being screamed at and threatened with a belt. My father standing over, telling me how I was only a failure and I will never amount to anything in my life. I really cannot continue to be scared of going to sleep. I have tried to reach out to people today, but I have been ignored. I guess people don't want anything to do with someone who suffers with severe mental health conditions.

This has made me feel alone again, a feeling I haven't felt for a few days. It's not a feeling I want and I really do not want to fall into a downward spiral of despair once again.

Last night, I was dreaming about keeping Leah-Jane safe. I was terrified of negative energy spreading on her. I keep dreaming that my father keeps trying to touch Leah-Jane in the way that he has touched Sabrina. These dreams always wake me up. I need to keep my daughter safe and it worries me so much. She is never going to step foot in that house as long as he is there. I cannot allow her to be at risk. I don't want to keep dreaming about this. Each night I go to bed with a happy thought in my mind, but it soon wears off, taking over my sub-consciousness. Trying to get the better of me and bring me down. I need to be strong. I need to protect my family and I must look after my daughter.

I have felt alone most of my life. Why should it matter now? I can remember coming home from school, walking alone and then sitting in my room. Only for the same thing to repeat itself every single day. I used to walk myself to school at a very young age. Mum and Dad, too busy to take me. Honestly, I can only ever remember one day where my dad took me to school.

It was always my own responsibility. Then, as I got older, Sabrina became my responsibility and when I finished secondary school, I would have to pick her from school too. Why was this put on me? Was it because Mum and Dad couldn't be bothered? Or because they were simply too busy? Many questions in my mind that I would like to have laid to rest.

This morning I saw beautiful pictures of the sun rising in Tenerife. Jade had shared them on Facebook. I looked at these photos, and they reminded me of the time I used to love watching the sunrise and the sunset over the waters on the south coast. It is something I truly miss. I miss the water, the sea, I miss it so much. When I was 21 years old, I was lonely and befriended a man called Sean who I met online. Sean was Irish and had Leukaemia. He was very sick; I used to go and visit him in the hospital to keep him company. He was so funny, never scared of what he was facing and always made me laugh. He spent most of his time in hospital poorly. One day, he told me he would love to see the sunset over the sea one last time. I made sure I could do this.

When Sean was feeling well enough, I drove him to the Solent where I used to park my car when I watched the sunset on my own. Sean was so happy, his smile beamed across his face. He got to watch the sunset with me which was a very happy moment in my life. Giving someone their incredible wish. Sean sadly passed away 3 weeks later. It was a very sad moment in my life. All I wanted was to keep a friend and to make someone else feel happy and cared about. I have never told anyone about Sean, not even Claire. Perhaps this moment has something to do with my mental health, I do not know. The loss of someone I cared about made me want to hide away forever. I didn't want to get close to anyone again as I was scared, I was going to lose them.

It's almost time I need to take Leah-Jane to school.

Today, I have it in my mind I cannot forget anything of hers. After this, I will come home for a bit and wait for the text from Greg. I am hoping to see Greg, my friend, today. Friends are so precious, and we need to keep them close to us. I have let too many friends drift away in the past. Was this because I was isolated when I was younger? Or is this because I just didn't know what a real friendship meant? I guess two questions only I know the answer to. When my mind is clearer, I will revisit these questions.

I have just got home from spending the day with Greg, his daughter, and his dog. This was the first time I had seen Greg's daughter, what a beautiful little girl she is. I can visualise her big, beaming eyes and a smile that could grow swaths of flowers. We started by going out for a walk around the local park and the woods. It felt nice to be outside again even though it was raining. I love walking around the nature to relax myself. We walked around for about 45 minutes before returning to Greg's home, we went into the lounge and played some video games. This was nice as I had not been into my gaming for about 2 years now. I used to love playing video games, but my interest in this has dwindled away. It was good to feel that experience again and perhaps I may get back into this.

We had a cup of tea and I had some melon. It was nice and refreshing, helped pick me up a bit. We then decided to play 2 board games, we played without my fear of someone breaking anything. I had a lovely time with Greg today and even though I still feel very unwell due to my lack of sleep, I feel happier in myself again. Friends, to me, are very important, and they help bring out a better version of me. Knowing that people care and are willing to spend time with me helps lift my self-esteem.

I have come home and Claire has got me a badge which says

"live your dream". I find this very sweet and I appreciate everything she does for me. I am hoping now to have a peaceful evening; one that isn't interrupted by horrible flashbacks from the past.

I remember not leaving school with the best grades. I think it was a bummer, but it hasn't stopped me from succeeding in my life outside of school. After school and college, I thought I would never go anywhere, that I was only going to struggle for the rest of my life. Both mentally and financially. It was wrong of me to self-loathe. I have since managed to complete my QCF level 3 in health and social care. I was so pleased when I achieved this. I felt my role in care was complete and that I was able to deliver the best possible care to anyone who I supported. I also have an NCFE level 3 in mental health and psychiatry. I feel this course is where I learned how to control my feelings and emotions better. I am sure learning about mental health helped me keep my emotions hidden behind me. Maybe it didn't. I don't know. What I know is, no matter how hard you try, you can only keep things hidden for so long. It felt as if I had rage filled in me; something decorous that wanted to burst out. It started to ring out of my eyes when I couldn't hold it in anymore; my breakdowns were brushing off my face to show the world I was suffering alone.

I also have a level 3 award in counselling. Perhaps I should have used this course to realise that I needed help sooner. I was so hell-bent, wanting to help others when I just couldn't put my own needs before. I have always wanted to support other people. But I should've known if I couldn't look after myself, how could I have possibly helped anyone else?

With the counselling course, I completed a level 3 award in cognitive behavioural therapy, again, all I wanted to do was feel better, help people overcome their struggles when inside I was struggling all along.

I have completed my TAQA level 3 in vocational learning. It means that I can assess anyone up to the same level of standards that I have in any qualification. I completed this alongside my level 5 diploma in leadership for health and social care and children and young people's services. I am now able to complete the assessments and can be an assessor for any of the courses that I have done. When I got this qualification, I felt a great sense of achievement. I felt I was at the top of my game, and I was moving up in my career and in my own life.

People ask me two questions. How have you managed to hold this in for so long? How could we not see that you are struggling? If I bring myself to explain my situation, I am coping with my mental illness by helping others. When I am focusing on someone else, it gives me a purpose and it helps take away my inner feelings. It increases my optimism and makes me feel alive. I love giving, I hate taking. I had learned to trick my mind into locking past events away in a vault in my brain. They were always there, and at times, small things would trigger some memories, but I was able to suppress these by thinking about the positives in life and focusing on my breathing. When I was struggling, I never let anyone see it. I was self-conscious and I would take myself away into a quiet room, be it home or work. My way of not allowing people to see me looking down, or signs I was struggling to hide from them until I could regain my composure to face people again. I always thought this was the best way of coping with my emotions. It wasn't, I know now after I've seen my anxiety take my life out of my palm twice. I have learned people don't judge you for being ill. My true friends and family have shown me that it's okay to not be okay. It's just not okay to keep things buried inside. I really cannot thank them enough for everything they do for me and continue to do for me. I feel blessed to have this small circle of people in my life.

Although today, I have not heard from my mum, this is the first day I have not heard from her since she visited over a week ago. Claire is mad at my mother, and when I asked why, she said my mum didn't do anything she was supposed to do. Instead, as a mother, she failed to see what was going on and did nothing about it when she figured. Claire says she feels my mum is equally at fault for the chaos ringing in my body.

When I actually come to think of it, I realise what Claire means. I guess, at times, I was too blind to blame my mother for any of this. Dad was the one loud and abusive, but Mum, she was inattentive.

I realise it now as I write this, I was not given what I needed from a mother; home-cooked meals, her warmth and embrace, a lively roof over my head, anything basic; she didn't pay attention. I can see how careless she all along was. Back in the late 1980's and 1990's, these issues were just never looked into by my mother even.

It also baffles me to know how my school never did anything for me. Or maybe, I should have done more to show my sufferings? Should I, again, take ownership and responsibility for not seeking help when I needed it the most? But, then again I was a child. Was this really my job? I honestly don't think it was. Claire is perfectly entitled to her opinions and I will always listen to Claire's views. She, as a mother herself, would absolutely do anything for her child and would always notice signs of withdrawal and neglect.

13.9.19 – SLEEP IS A BLESSING!

WHAT DO I HAVE TO DO TO FIX THE HURT IN MY EYES, what can I do to shut my heart?

I am trying to understand why I am struggling to sleep. Last night, I was exhausted, worn out, and sick to my core. I even went to bed at 22:10 to try and get some sleep. How wrong could I be? It was the 10th night and my sleep was more disturbed than ever. Waking up in a frenzy, shaking, sweaty; struggling to breathe. Anxiety taking over my mind and my sub-consciousness consumed by my thoughts of misery. Why do my nightmares consume me? I am guessing I have to accept this is not going to be a fast and easy fix. I spoke to the doctor about my sleep, but instead, I was told they couldn't prescribe me certain medications anymore. So, I guess this is down to me and it should be figured out. I am only on my second day of meditation that won't be effective yet. After the school run, I will be going to the pharmacy to see if there is anything that can be bought over the counter that will help with my sleep.

I took Leah-Jane to school, she was very sweet this morning and wanted lots of cuddles throughout the morning, and it made me smile. I felt so loved by her this morning. She went to school with a huge smile on her face and told me that she is looking forward to school. I am so glad she is enjoying school. I never want her to hate school like I did. I never want her to feel the dread and daily pain of getting up for school in the morning. The sun has been shining all morning and it is a very beautiful day.

I have been to the pharmacy this morning to see if there is anything organic I can try that will help me sleep at night. I have managed to buy some valerian root extract, hoping it is going to work as it is mainly used to help with the relief of sleep disturbances. I really do want to be able to sleep again. I don't want another night where I sleep for an hour and wake up with the sweats, shaking. I am going to try this tonight to see how I get on. I have nothing left to lose anymore.

The last time I remember struggling to sleep was 2014. It was June and I had just come home from work and the neighbour was outside his house tending to his motorbike. As I got to my door, he shouted to me,

"Do you know why I had the police here this morning ready to smash my door in. I have a baby for fuck's sake in there," I told him I had absolutely no idea what he was talking about as I had been at work. He told me how the police had told him one of his neighbours had reported him for selling drugs and that it could have only been us or the house next to his. I unlocked the door and went into the house. I told Claire what he had said to me, and she told me how the police had been around the area this morning, but she didn't know what for. I told her I think this guy feels it's us who reported him. Claire said she wasn't having that and went out to talk to him. She came back in after a few minutes and said that he was quiet.

We saw them from time to time over the next month and him and his partner ignored us and didn't speak to us at all. I went to work on a Saturday in early July and when I came home, I saw my mother-in-law was there with Claire. I asked what was wrong as Claire looked distressed. She told me that she was in the garden putting the washing on the line. He then came into his gardens pacing up and down with a letter in his hand. Claire asked him if he was okay. He then shouted at Claire, telling her it was us who grassed him up. He became quite threatening and said the letter said it was us. He threatened Claire.

Eventually, his partner came out and shouted at him and told him to go inside. She then shouted at Claire, too. Claire told me Leah-Jane was in the garden at the time. I was so angry and I wanted to confront him, but Claire asked me not to.

As time went on, I struggled to sleep and I began feeling anxious about him when it read in the newspaper how he had been in prison for violently attacking a family with his friend a few years prior. It scared me because I knew how he wouldn't have any sympathy for anyone, he could do anything not realising his actions and wouldn't care for people. I trapped myself in my house, and I was very on edge when I left for work. Or when I was coming back home from work.

He didn't work and would pop in and out of his house all day. The chances of bumping into him were high. I became withdrawn and really started to struggle with my sleep. We put our house on the market to sell. We didn't want to live next door to this person. He was vile and terrifying to be around. Whenever we saw him, he would just stare at us with such a cold stare. He would push his chest out to try and be intimidating. I never looked him in the eye. I chose to look away from him.

A HUGE ESCAPE

Step out, look for an escape, you may not find it right there, but push through to reach where you have to.

In August, we went on holiday to Gran Canaria for 2 weeks. I did feel like it was an escape, but it brought with itself a lot of ease. It was nice being far away and not feeling scared to leave the house for any reason. We had such a lively holiday and explored much of the island.

We went and saw dolphins and fin whales in the sea. Leah-Jane did her party trick and fell asleep like she always does when we go see the dolphins. We went to the entertainment every night and visited the local town quite regularly. We all felt free away from the evil that was lurking next door. Unfortunately, after two weeks, we had to return home. We were both hoping he had moved out as he had said,

"you don't need to worry about me anymore as we are moving," to Claire when he shouted at her.

We arrived home late August and he was still there. I could hear him through the walls most nights with his friends being very loud and calling us horrible names. The walls were thin in that terraced house and you could usually hear everything. I used to keep so quiet. I didn't want him to hear me. We even had the TV turned down low to make sure he couldn't hear that. We didn't want him to notice us at all. We both felt so ill all the time, scared to take the bins out, open the front door. You should never be made to feel like that in your own house. We even had neighbours come round to talk to us because he had abused them. They called him our druggie neighbour.

It was mid-September; I was leaving the house to pick Leah-Jane from school. As I went to open the front door, I saw his door opening in the reflection of the house opposite. I closed my door and locked it. I waited 5 minutes, opened the door, and as I started to walk, he came out of his house and called me back. He asked me,

"Why have you got a letter from social services, what the fuck are you doing?",

"I don't know what you're talking about", I replied.

"You're lucky that I am going to prison, because if I wasn't, I'd fucking smack you", pausing for a bit,

"you're fucked anyway it won't be me doing it", he had said. It scared me as I was threatened to be attacked. I told him I didn't want any trouble and that I wanted a quiet life. He told me it was us who reported him to the police because we reported the previous residents, too. Which, obviously, was bullshit because we had never reported him. The school behind the houses reported him as children were found with drugs, and they spilled the information on him. I never told him this because what would it have done. His partner then came out and told him to go away, telling me she is not a bad mum and that just because he likes drugs doesn't mean she is bad. I listened to this for a few minutes then managed to get away to get Leah-Jane from school.

I didn't want to return home after this and I called my mother-in-law and asked her if we could all stay with them for a while. She told me to just ring the police. In my head, it wouldn't have solved everything. But I knew it would just make him angrier, and he may end up coming back with an even bigger fuss. In the end, I told Claire I couldn't stay in that house tonight. We booked a hotel in Hyde and stayed there for the night. We started to live away following that day.

In November 2014, he and Claire ended up having an incident in between. Claire was on her way home from work. The neighbour was about to turn out of the road in his car, he was staring at her with a cold stare that she told him to

"fuck off". He reversed his car and turned the car towards her whilst she was on the pavement. Claire said she moved, and he drove off down the road. Claire had always said she found this traumatic, but when Claire told me about this day, I felt strangely very angry. We had always said we should have gone to the police, but we couldn't do so while living there; things could have just gotten a lot worse.

We couldn't manage to sell our house, so we took it off the market. We went down the landlord route and decided to let it out. We eventually found a small house that we liked in a quieter area with parking. We placed an offer which got accepted. Then, the checks started, it was getting close to Christmas, and we were both on the edge and wanted to move in as quickly as possible. December 16th, 2014 came, our moving day and oh, we were so delighted to be doing this.

Our moving day went well. We had 3 men helping with the removals and my friend to help as well. I took Leah-Jane to school and came back. When I came back, my friend told me that the removal men needed the neighbour to move his car. When they knocked on his door the neighbours said

"good riddance to the grasses, we drove them out" he did move his car, but his comment made him look stupid. One of the delivery men said he was just a runt; give him a good slap, and he will leave you alone. This made me laugh. He kept out of the way whilst we moved. When we were all set and done, getting into the car to move, he opened his window and shouted

"good riddance grasses, and by the way, I have your national insurance number", but I couldn't care less anymore, we were out of his sight.

It took me and Claire a very long time to get over the sounds of a motorbike he used. For the first few months, I would see him in the local town on his bike. If he ever saw my car, he would stop his bike and just stare at it. I had enough of this and would just stare right back at him. Eventually, we changed our car and I didn't see him for about 4 years.

I never want to live in a house with an experience like that again. Home should be where you feel safe and relaxed, not where you feel threatened and on edge. People always say a house should be welcoming and caring, which, my old house wasn't. It was a horrible experience parking up at that house. Scared to get out of your car. Not knowing who could be there waiting for you. I am so grateful for where I live now as everyone around here has been fantastic.

UNWIND, RELAX!

Today, I am curling my hands in the breaths of winds moving me, it is a sunlit, clear day. It urged me to follow the checklist Jade had made for me. I had to go for a walk and track a few miles. So, I decided to walk down the main road and into the woods. I love this walk as it follows the river. It's a very peaceful walk and one that I have completed many times in the past. The last time I did the full circular was about a year ago. When I got to the woods, it was so quiet, not a person in sight. I could hear the water flowing down the river. The sounds of the birds chirping was complete bliss. I walked through the woods and out round the back of the next town. I continued back into the woods following the river for a few miles. It was lovely. There were muddy areas, but it didn't faze me. I was in nature. I was in my element. I was doing what I loved. I feel I may have rekindled my love for walking again. As I continued to walk through the woods, I came out on the main road by the garden centre. The last part of my journey was a walk down the roads and then back round to the house. The walk was 5.4 miles. I completed this in an hour and 29 minutes. This was the fastest I had completed this walk. I am proud of myself for getting the house and being motivated to go for a nice long walk.

Our fundraising team wanted another challenge, and

in Match 2014, we arranged to complete the Hadrian's Wall walk over a 4-day period. When the time arrived in the summer, I was anxious about going. As I was leaving Leah-Jane and Claire for 4 days with the horrible neighbour next door.

Claire insisted that I go and complete the challenge. I was picked up from home by the driver the day before we started the challenge. We drove up to Newcastle Upon-Tyne where our adventure would begin. The following morning it was bright and early, we got driven to the start point. Then the adventure began.

The journey started in Wallsend just outside Newcastle city centre. We had to walk through a housing estate and then parallel to the Tyne, heading into the city centre. It was a lovely hot day and the sun was shining. It wasn't long before we were out of the city centre and 15 miles down the road to Heddon on the wall. My ankle started to hurt when we reached Heddon and my boots were sore. I swapped shoes with someone else. We continued our journey and met with the driver who gave me my trainers, so I could wear these for the walk. We continued to walk for many many miles, eventually coming onto a pub where we stopped for a drink. The campsite was only a few miles from here, and we camped overnight ready for day 2.

Day 2 was awful, the weather was poor, it was raining, dark, and very wet. This part of the journey was very hilly. Lots of climbing and descending throughout the day. After 11 hours of intense walking, we did not make it to the hostel where we were staying. We were out of daylight, and we were 2 miles from our destination. We called our driver who picked us up and took us to the hostel. We settled in and then went to the pub for a few drinks. After going to bed, we got up bright and early, had breakfast and then went back to where we stopped the previous day.

Day 3 was the longest day of walking. We started walking at 9AM, 2 miles behind schedule. We knew we had an ultra-marathon to complete today. The first part of the day was very hilly, but soon the terrain levelled out and you could see parts of where Hadrian's Wall used to be. Eventually, we came across the wall. We continued to walk and walk, and we didn't stop for lunch. We pressed on and at this point, my feet were burning, and I was getting blisters. I was given some cushioned blister plasters when we stopped and the driver helped tend to the injuries. But this didn't stop us, we soldiered on pushing harder than we had pushed before. We reached the campsite just after 9pm, all after 12 hours of solid walking. We rested for the night and had dinner.

Come morning and it was our last day of the challenge. We were all prepared to finish this challenge. My blisters had gotten worse and both soles of my feet were covered. I knew I had to do this no matter what. We started the morning and it wasn't long before we were in Carlisle; the last day, however, was a nice flat day. No hills and simple flats. It wasn't long before we knew we were coming towards the end of our journey. My feet were so sore. I could barely walk. The driver then told us it was the last mile and to give it everything. I could barely stand, my feet were blistered and hurt. I pushed and pushed and made it to the end of the 82-mile journey. I wish I had the correct footwear for this. I used motor racing shoes with no cushion or protection. What a fool I was.

When we completed the challenge, I felt a huge sense of achievement. I had collected all my stamps along the route, so I knew I could send off for my medal. When we got back to the bus, I just collapsed into my seat. We began the journey back. I remember we stopped at a service station, I went to the toilet, but I could barely walk. I couldn't put pressure on my feet. The pain was so intense. A gentleman in the toilets asked me if I was okay, I told him I was. I managed to eventually get myself back on the bus and went back home. Only to have to go to the doctors the following day to have dressings applied to my feet. It took almost 2 months for the blisters on their bottom of my feet to completely disappear. Would I do this challenge again? Yes, I would in a heartbeat, but over 2 days and with the right footwear.

Tonight, my schedule told me to take Leah-Jane out after school. I told her this before school. Oh boy, did she remember. Soon as I picked her up, she told me how we are supposed to have fun this afternoon. I brought her home and I decided to take her out for dinner. I could see the warm embrace in her eyes as she enjoyed her meal. She was very happy, telling me all about what she was learning at school. It was a nice meal, and I am glad I have done this. By the night, it is now about unwinding and relaxing. I am going to watch some shows and I am going to relax my mind. I am not going to think about sleep, I am not going to allow my mind to wander.

14.9.19 – THE WRONG ROAD

STILL, I SIT WITH THE SAME REOCCURRING THOUGHTS blurring my mind, still, I run after an escape that only takes me back in time.

Last night I had alcohol, something I regret doing to myself. I couldn't take any sleeping pills because they put off with my medications. I thought drinking would help me sleep a little better, and oh, how wrong could I be. I couldn't control the trauma my nightmares were bringing to me because of the drink. I woke up having a huge panic attack, struggling to breathe, I couldn't think; all I could feel was pain. I felt pain as if I was being struck with a belt buckle. It had never even happened to me. Yet I was in my dreams, being beaten with a belt. Why would I dream of something like it? It was horrible. I tried to go back to sleep only to have horrible dreams of falling, just falling from the sky. In the end, I gave up trying to sleep. It has now been 11 nights with little to no sleep. I really am starting to feel the toll physically. My focus is gone and my mind just floats away into a world of limbo.

Where do I go from this now? I have tried meditation, but it has only been 3 days. I will continue with this in the hope that this is the answer to finally getting some sleep. I don't want to rely on medications to help me sleep. I want to find a way to manage my sleep for the long term. There will be a way, I just have to find my way.

Let's go back to 2001, when I was 15 years old, I was sitting in my room playing video games with my brother. It was a nice evening, and we were having a laugh. It begun to get late, around 23:45, Mum and Dad came home from the pub playing darts. Mum was clearly very angry with Dad. Dad was very drunk and couldn't stand up straight. He couldn't get his words out properly either. Something must have happened when they were out. But I do not know what this was. Dad started to become loud towards Mum, his tone loudened as he increasingly felt agitated. Then, out of nowhere, Mum lost her temper. I remember she punched Dad so hard in his face he fell backwards into my bedroom on the floor. He tried to get up, but Mum pushed his head into the drawer of my wardrobe. The drawer was already damaged and wouldn't close. The force of the push crumbled the drawer. Mum continued to hit Dad, making his face bleed.

I wonder how I watched that; we hadn't ever seen our mum this aggressive before. We were worried she would continue hitting Dad. We didn't want getting in trouble or Dad hurting. It was scary, we were shaking, but we had to do something. We couldn't stand watching it, none of us liked fighting; verbally or physically, in any way. We had to stop Mum. Robert and I managed to stop Mum soon as we started shouting, then, she left the room. Dad got up and went to bed. It was the last argument that night and the first time I had seen my mum fight back.

Today, I feel it was the end for her. She had had enough of the abuse she had received from Dad over the years. The following morning, Mum was very quiet. She didn't speak much. Dad came downstairs around 10:00AM, face all battered and bruised. He asked what had happened last night as his head was hurting, and he felt unwell. Mum told him he pushed her too far, she had to give him what he deserved. They didn't speak after this, not for the rest of the day. But, the following day, things got back to normal, and they both went out to darts again. It was just a vicious circle; the drinking, the arguments. They never stopped for long.

I hated seeing my family argue. I just wanted a nice, caring family, not the family upheaval my parents always sent our way. I assume my parents thought it was okay to scream, abuse, and manipulate people.

I may not be perfect, I am far from it, but I have instilled in me some traits my parents forced me to, which only drives me away from people and out of my life. I didn't want this happening, there is no way I would have allowed drinking, arguments, or physical fights in my house. There is no way I'd want Leah-Jane subjected to the hell I was when I was growing up. My experiences have transformed me differently in many ways. At times, I can be defensive and argumentative, but I have been working to improve it. I have a lot of support from people close to my heart. But then, I can also be extremely compassionate and caring, which again, is my favourite trait. I love helping others, being there for others, and I will always continue to do.

This morning, I went to the barber. I hadn't been to the barbers in almost 6 years. I went to get my hair cut and have my beard groomed. I would usually just shave all my hair off and shave my beard down to thin stubble. Not anymore. I felt good as I got my haircut. I know too many people who do this often, but I am not one of them. However now, I try my best to care for myself. It was a huge step forward for me to grow my self-confidence. In a very long time, for the first time, I have spent time caring about my appearance. I feel good, for once, feel I look the best so far.

After I had been to the barber, I had one other thing to do; to sell the ring my father got me for my 19th birthday. I want to get rid of anything he has given me, the ring was the first thing to go. I walked into the jewellers' outlet, I wasn't hoping to get any money for this ring, perhaps only £15. I was surprised when I was offered £55. I accepted this offer; I was in two minds of what to do with this money. Destroy it, donate it to charity, or spend it on myself. After I talked to Claire, we decided it wasn't money from my father, it was money that had been given to me by a jeweller. With this mind-set, I decided to treat myself, I saw a pair of trainers I really liked and decided why not? I'm feeling more confident today and looking forward to the rest of my day.

It was February 2010. Claire was pregnant with Leah-Jane, I lived in Hedge End, and Claire lived in Manchester. There was no way we could continue this long distance relationship with a child on the way. I knew it wasn't a decision favourable for the two of us and our baby. Claire was a secondary school teacher. A professional with a very good job and her own house. I was a healthcare assistant in the mental health unit. I lived with my parents. The last thing I wanted for myself and Claire was to call her to live around my parents.

I chose to move to Manchester with Claire. I resigned from my job and received a letter from them thanking me for my service with them.

I remember my last day working in mental health. Everyone was really nice to me, and they all told me they would miss me. I remember going home from work and mum asking me to go to the pub with her. I was a bit hesitant as I was tired and had a long drive the following day. But I went over the pub where I was greeted by my former colleagues and was absolutely spoilt with gifts. I never expected anything from them, at least not the gifts I received. I thanked everyone, had a drink with them, and then went home. The following day, I loaded my car and journeyed to Manchester. I could not fit everything I had in my car, so I knew I had to go back. I stayed the weekend with Claire and went back to Hedge End on Monday morning. I spent my last week in that house, totally hating it.

Claire's house was very clean, she lived in a peaceful area. The last day in the house was incredible, I was free to leave and I didn't have to live there anymore. No more horrible smells. No more broken walls, furniture, and no more filth. I didn't have to listen to arguments or see my parents fight anymore. It was nice to know freedom was coming my way. I loaded my car with the last of my items and completed the 230+ mile journey to Manchester. I have never looked back. I have visited that house since, but I have not stayed overnight. If we visit, we book hotels.

I remember visiting once with Claire and Leah-Jane. Leah-Jane was about 3 years old. She went into the living room and asked my mum and dad why there was a hole in the ceiling in the living room. My dad told Leah-Jane that it was to let the smoke out of the room. Both my parents were smokers and you could clearly see the nicotine stains on the walls and ceilings in the whole house. The hole was grotty, with water dripping down. Mum said a pipe had burst. I asked her why did she not get it repaired, again, the only excuse was

"down to money." I took Leah-Jane upstairs, she wanted to use the toilet, next to it, and there was another hole that went directly to the kitchen below.

Leah-Jane didn't use the toilet when she saw this and I personally don't blame her. I did not feel at ease myself using this toilet. It was a grotty mess of a house, with no handles on the doors, garden overgrown, and the back door seriously damaged. The toilet was leaking. I was so embarrassed to have Claire and Leah-Jane see this. These were the conditions I had to daily live in as I was growing up.

To realise how I had spent years growing up in such a house, I think I was very patient. What worries me now is how my nieces and nephews would have to put up with the awful smell of the house. I don't want them to get bullied in school the way I was. I would hate for anyone else and I mean anyone to suffer in silence the way I did throughout school. It was one of the hardest times of my life and when I think about it, it brings me to my knees with nothing but emotions of despair and pain.

Moving to Manchester was one of the scariest things I had ever done. I didn't know anyone. I had no friends up here. The only person I knew was my partner Claire. It was intimidating. I didn't have any work lined up, and I was about to have a blessing that is my child. I took a few months off from work which was my choice, to give my mind some time to relax.

I started to explore Manchester and learned a lot about its culture and history. When I visit new places, I like to learn about its history, something I have always been interested in. When I started to apply for work, things moved very quickly, I was offered interviews right away. I was offered many posts in different places. In one day, I had 3 interviews. I gave many different interviews, but I wanted something that would bring the best out of me.

After considering a lot, one of the only job offers clicked my heart, it was the one I chose and I still work here to this day.

So today, another good thing that happened is, I received a video game Claire had bought for me. I am hoping I will be able to play this with Greg online, get an old hobby back, and have some fun once again. I really hope for it to distract my mind from the thoughts that have been consuming me throughout my life. I look forward to trying this out. Will it be tonight that I will finally sleep? I have yet to find, but it'll definitely happen sooner or later, and I am looking forward to unwind and have some stress relief.

Today, I fell asleep in the afternoon for about 40 minutes. I hadn't slept in the day for a few months now. It was actually nice to have what they call a cat nap. It may have not been for long, but I managed to sleep. I don't recall falling asleep. But I do recall waking up, the good part of my sleep was that there weren't any dreams. No memories, nothing. I don't remember a single thing from it. It has relaxed me; it gives me hope that tonight I will be able to sleep and I will be able to rest without fear of the past coming into my dreams and haunting me. I have listened to music all day. The television hasn't been on. It's been nice to just reflect and listen to music. Something I strongly recommend to anyone who is suffering with mental health issues. Music has a unique way of relaxing my mind. It closes off my surroundings and my thoughts become the lyrics.

Sometimes I just listen to sounds of nature. My love for nature is so strong. It's one true passion of mine. Being so far away from the sea can make me feel emotional at times. This was always my safe place in the past. Having the sounds of the waves play all around me whilst I close my eyes is incredibly relaxing. It's like I'm there again. Back in my safe zone with water all around me.

What is it with the sea? Why does the sea relax me so much? I spent 23 years of my life living around water or near to water. I always found it so therapeutic. I used to love walking along the coast with my bare feet in the shallows, allowing the waves to touch my toes, the feeling of the cool sea was bliss. Something I miss so dearly. When I look back at it, it makes me realise I need to visit the sea more. Something that I will aim to do throughout the rest of the year. It doesn't have to be sunny and hot for me to enjoy the sea. I have enjoyed it in all sorts of weathers. The sounds, the smell, the feeling of it takes my mind into a comfort zone. All the worries and thoughts around me disappear. It's amazing how Mother Nature can be such an incredible stress reliever.

Tonight, after I took a bath, I got out and was hit with an intense wave of feeling incredibly low. I sat downstairs on the sofa, and I was feeling immensely down. I had texted my mother because she said my father never came home last night. I asked her if he had come home since, and she told me he hadn't. She said he might be working at Goodwood, which is just an assumption.

I got really worried and my thoughts started to put me away. Why was I so worried that my dad hadn't come home? Should I really even care? He is still my dad for a fact, and I feel worried for him. Even though I want to disown him, it's not that easy. I guess it's my nature of not wanting any harm to come to anyone, but not knowing his whereabouts made me have horrible thoughts. I felt the urge to do something to myself. It took every ounce of strength that I have left in me to fight this. I didn't get up from the sofa.

I wouldn't allow my thoughts and emotions to get the better of me. I focused on the positives in life, not the negatives and I managed to fight off the temptation of self-harm.

There are, however, times when my illness tries to take over my mind. It tries to make me feel I cannot cope anymore. I am not going to let it win and I will fight this. I feel today the battle has been in my favour. How many more battles will I have to endure? I guess I must continue to fight for myself, my family, and my friends. I feel I am now learning how to fight this through. I'm trying new approaches. I'm not trying to bottle it up anymore. I'm going to make sure I take all the support I have been given and not feel alone anymore. I know I'm not alone anymore. I have the best support I could have asked for. I just wish I had asked for support sooner, the stigma I felt kept me from it. I was too ashamed of people and what they would think of me, but people have been amazing, which I will always be grateful for.

15.9.19 – MY DAD HAUNTS ME!

Last night I thought I'd sleep well again, I went to bed early, but it didn't take long for my nightmares to return. The first nightmare I had was about my dad. He was strangling me; he was taking every last breath out of my body. I couldn't breathe, it was horrible. In my dream, I passed out because of being violently strangled, strangled for reasons I do not know. I woke up at 02:15AM, I was struggling to breathe. I remember seeing the time on my phone. I was in a panic, gasping for breath. The dream felt so real. It felt like I was going to die.

I managed to fall asleep again after about 30 minutes. My next dream was extremely bizarre. I was walking through the woods and a giant serpent came out of the trees and started to constrict me. It was crushing me to death, taking all the air out of my lungs. I was helpless and couldn't do anything to stop this serpent. The serpent then opened its mouth and begun to eat me. In the same moment, I woke up sweating heavy. This is not something that I have ever dreamed of before. Not something I have ever thought about. I do not fear serpents. I like them. So, what does this dream mean? Does it have something to do with me feeling suffocated by my thoughts and emotions?

MY GRANDPARENTS WERE NOTHING LIKE DAD

I think, one person, just one person close to you will pour their bright shine on you if you just offer your hand to them.

I want to talk about my grandparents, my dad's parents. They used to live in a small bungalow in Hamble near the sea. My grandparents were a lot of fun. I used to love visiting them. It was the only time I would get to have tea or coffee. They used to have dogs too. A Chihuahua who I remember throughout my early childhood. He sadly passed away when I was young. They then got a King Charles spaniel who was amazing. He loved lots of cuddles and going for walks with my granddad. My grandmother was born in 1934, she was Scottish, my grandfather was born in 1933, and he was also Scottish. They met each other in a fish market in Aberdeen in the late 1940's. They were together for over 55 years, married 52 of those years. My grandmother was short in height, fair, had quite a temper, and was a smoker. She was amazing to be around. We would take her out shopping. We would take her to clubs. As long as I can remember, I do not ever remember her having a job. Her health did deteriorate very quickly. I remember having to push her around in a wheelchair in the last days of her life.

A wonderful memory I have is of their 50th wedding

anniversary. It was celebrated in a local social club. The fantastic memory of this occasion was that everyone from the family was there. Relatives from Scotland, London, United States, and Canada. It was the first time in my life I was in a gathering where everyone was together. Sadly, it was also the last time I was to experience this. It was lovely having the family together. It was lovely to spend time with relatives I had never seen before. Many of whom I didn't even know existed.

My grandmother and grandfather were very happy this day. I can still remember their smiles to this day.

There were many more amazing memories. There was this old World War 2 gun on the beach at Hamble. I used to play there with my brother Robert when I was young. We used to run around the fort having a laugh. My grandparents used to love taking us there. They used to love seeing the smile on our faces as we were running around and playing. I don't know if the big gun is still there.

Maybe one day I will revisit this location in hope that it can bring back some warm-hearted memories of my grandparents.

In late 2004, my grandmother fell really sick, she had suffered multiple heart attacks and spent a lot of time in the hospital. She then got obstructive jaundice that worsened her situation more. Eventually, she was bedridden in 2005. It was her wish to pass away in her own home, but her situation didn't allow, her daughters had to shift her to the hospital. My mum was very upset with this because she wanted to follow my grandmothers wishes, but my mum did not have any say in it as she was not my grandmother's daughter.

I never got to see my grandmother in her last few months because she had asked our parents to not bring us to see her. I really wish I was given the opportunity to say goodbye to my grandmother, I love her so very much.

Sadly, my grandmother passed away in mid-2005 at the age of 71. It was a very sad moment. I remember my dad not saying anything. He was quiet, and he didn't show any emotions. He just kept himself to himself.

I remember my mum being very upset. She would spend hours crying. My grandfather, he didn't know how to react, he had just lost his wife, his soulmate. The woman who he had shared his entire life with. The day of the funeral came, the service was very respectful and my grandmother was laid to rest. Her ashes were given to my father, her wish to be scattered in the sea in Aberdeen. Something my father has still not done to this day. My grandmother sits on a shelf in his living room. The other half of her ashes scattered on my cousin's graves in London.

My grandfather had a wicked sense of humour. He has a very deep Scottish accent and nobody could understand what he would be saying. My dad would usually act as the translator. My grandad was social. He liked whisky and cream soda at his local club. He wasn't a regular drinker, and he didn't smoke. He had love for dogs and loved going for walks with his dogs.

I don't ever remember my grandfather working, but he used to tell me stories about working on the fish markets.

He was a very proud man, and he deeply cared for his children.

After the death of my grandmother, he became very subdued and quiet. He was lost without her.

After a while, he started to go out again and started to talk to people. He continued to live alone in Hamble, then he met another woman. Someone who understood his grief and listened to him, after a few years of talking and getting along he moved to Eastleigh with her. This woman was amazing, she clearly cared about my grandfather, and I was happy that he was no longer alone anymore.

Leah-Jane used to love seeing her granddad, he loved seeing Leah-Jane, it was fantastic to have Leah-Jane meet her great-grandfather, she never got the opportunity to meet her great-grandmother.

The last time I saw my grandfather was February 2016. He had been diagnosed with a stage 4 lung cancer. He told me he knew that he didn't have much time left and that he wasn't scared of dying. He told me death is a part of living and that we should never fear it, but embrace being back to the ones we have lost in the past. For the first time in a long time, he told me he missed his wife. I knew when he was looking forward to reunite with her in the afterlife.

I returned back home to Manchester. I was due to work a long weekend in June; I took a phone call from my aunt. She informed me that my grandfather was in hospital and that things did not look good. I did not hesitate. I got in my car, dragging Claire and Leah-Jane along and drove straight down to the hospital. I dropped

Leah-Jane off to Sabrina. I and Claire went to the hospital to see my grandfather. When I arrived, he was gaunt. He was not in his consciousness and was on a morphine driver. I knew it was the end when I saw him.

We sat with him the whole night. In the early hours, he gave his last breath and passed away. My aunts became very upset, my Dad just walked out the room. I went after my father to talk to him. I told him his sisters needed him. He walked back into the room to see them but didn't stay. He glanced over to look at his Dad and left for a cigarette.

I don't think my father has ever properly grieved over the loss of his parents. Maybe he doesn't know how to grieve. He has never spoken of them to me since their passing.

My grandfather passed away in June 2016, aged 83 years. His funeral was held 2 weeks later. I really miss him so much. I don't feel I have been able to grieve properly. A few months later, I was given the sad news that the lady he spent the last few years of his life with passed away, too. It was sad because I knew she deeply cared for my grandfather. The saying that you can die of a broken heart may be true.

AM I STUCK?

I have been looking forward to today. I, Claire and Leah-Jane are going to the Lake District to see our friends. It has been a few months since we had seen them and with everything going on, it was a really nice idea. We left home just after 11:00PM and reached around 12:30PM. When we reached, it was lovely to see them and the dogs.

We had a nice hot drink and then went to see some art festivals.

When we got to the first art festival, some of the rooms were busy. It started to make me feel dizzy. I am still not comfortable with strangers. The rooms were small and the smell of paints was strong. The art was lovely to look at, but inside I was struggling with the lack of space and the busy environments. It wasn't a comfortable experience for me.

The second location was no different. It was a small room with multiple stands displaying art, I again struggled with the busy environment and I really couldn't cope. I went outside. Then, we went for lunch, order what I wanted for lunch, a cheeseburger and chips.

Claire eventually came over with an annual pass for me to sign for the zoo. I thought this was odd as this zoo is very far away from home. Claire then told me she had paid £75 to adopt a snow leopard for me. It immediately upset me. Claire has been buying me things all week and I do not want things being bought for me. It makes me feel like a charity case and it make me feel really sick. I couldn't eat all of my lunch. Adopting an animal isn't something I would normally do. I would just donate the money for them. I don't get why Claire thought this would be a good idea. It feels like she is trying to cheer me up by buying me gifts. Things I don't want and things I don't need. Money is not making me happy. I told Claire I wasn't happy with this and it was a lot of money. I told her buying me things isn't going to make me happy. Claire said she understood this.

Am I being ungrateful? Many people would say

"yes you are", but the constant purchasing of things has triggered me. I don't want people to buy me things to try and cheer me up. I want people to just listen, talk, and try and understand how I am feeling from the inside. Claire kept trying to mention this to me and I just didn't want to talk about it anymore. I asked her to leave me alone, which only just upset her.

Am I being unreasonable? More than likely yes. But I really felt low because of it and I don't want people to feel that they have to buy things to make me happy. It was difficult after this as I didn't know what to say to Claire. I kept myself closed up and I'm feeling very fed up by myself. Maybe I should have just said thank you and accepted this. But, if I had let her continue buying me gifts, it would have only made me feel worse.

What I was hoping to be a good day turned out to be a very difficult day, not just for me, but for Claire too. I really didn't want to socialise after this and I began to close up. I don't want to become difficult. I just want people to understand what is going through my head.

Am I reacting this way because I never really got gifts as a child, perhaps that is the answer? I guess from now I'll stop trying to have amazing days, I will just start to face whatever is thrown in my direction. This way I cannot feel disappointed, and I won't disappoint anyone else.

I feel I spend so much time worrying about how other people are feeling. But does anyone ever really think about how I am feeling? I am beginning to notice that its human nature to be very selfish and think of how each of us are feeling. I have always done everything I can to help people who feel down to see how much positive they have in life.

I love helping others feel better and I love to help them learn to love themselves. Just with this process, I think I forgot I needed to see myself too.

Does anyone really care about how I am feeling? I just don't know. I want to believe that they do. I just don't feel this anymore. I feel alone again, lost in my own mind. This is a viscous circle for me at the moment. I just don't see a way out of this.

16.9.19 – ENOUGH!

I AM TAKING STEPS, ONE BREATH A MOMENT. I WILL cut through and I will direct my life where I want, not where the world will push me.

I went to bed last night to sleep. It was 22:20PM. But, I got a text from Greg asking if I wanted to play some video games online. I was wide awake and I decided to get up and play some games with him for a short while. It was nice to be playing online again. We played until about 00:00. After this I decided to go to bed, I got into bed and I just could not doze off. My mind was worried so much about what I was going to dream of.

I managed to fall asleep around 03:00AM only to wake after about 90 minutes in a cold sweat. The nightmares had returned, my father was there standing over my bed with his belt in his hand ready to hit me. I remember waking up before he could raise his hand to hit me. I hate having these dreams, I hate being unable to control my mind whilst I am asleep.

I miraculously managed to fall asleep again after this

for a few hours. I couldn't clear my subconscious, all I could hear was abusive language and shouting.

The previous night I was having dreams of a giant serpent crushing me and trying to devour me. I did some research into this and I found out the potential meaning of a serpent in your dreams.

It usually directs that we feel restricted somewhere in life, it can symbolise threat, tension, or resistance that I experience in my life that needs to be acknowledged. I now understand the meaning of this for me. With everything that is going on around me, no wonder I am having unusual dreams. I do feel trapped. I feel that the little boy inside me is trapped and wants to be laid to rest. A childhood ruined by abuse, one that needs to be set free into a world of positive energy.

I am feeling quite anxious today. I am seeing the doctor at 10:30AM. I feel that my mental health has not made any progress in the last week, instead, it has gradually been getting worse. I'm worried that I am going to need to have my medications increased. Maybe having them increased is a good thing? I will know when I will meet my doctor.

Claire is taking the day off work today to come with me. Last week I went alone and I struggled with this. I know I need support and I have to ensure that I continue to use all the support that I have available to me. I'm trying to keep myself focused. I'm thinking of positive things. I'm hoping my thoughts can help overcome all the negative energy that is consuming my physical presence.

I went to the doctors today and explained about my lack of sleep and that it has been 12 nights. I spoke about my dreams and nightmares. She was very understanding and gave me 3 tablets to try and help me to sleep to get some release from the exhaustion. I will try this tonight and I shall see how I get on with it. I am hoping I will get some rest tonight.

She was pleased with my progress, though. The lack of suicidal thoughts and the ability to stop myself from self-harming.

She feels I am going in the right direction. I can finally believe I am truly winning now, that it may still be a long fight. I can still get past it, with more strength and resilience than ever. I will see her again now in 2 weeks. I have come back feeling better and a lot more confident. I hope I can continue to instil this positive energy in me.

I never thought reaching out for help would serve me so well. I always thought people would belittle me for not being a tough man, for not getting on with my life. However, the overwhelming support I received from the doctor, medical professionals, family, and friends really pushed me to get better. It has given me a hope that there are many people out there who are kind-hearted, who listen to empathise and not judge.

As a teenager, I self-harmed for the first time. I was in school, struggling so much with the unwanted bullied and harassment for being smelly. I was sitting in woodwork class. I reached out for my pencil case, took a sharpener out, and started breaking the plastic off of it. I uncovered the blade and cut my arm. I think I liked how I felt in that moment, my skin tingling with a sensation that numbed my hurt. My mind was only focused on the blood and sting from the blade. I wanted to feel that physical pain. I didn't want my mind to be focused on feeling low and down. I wanted my mind to notice the pain. I wanted to think of something else other than the bullying and the pain that was going through my heart. I didn't cut myself hard the first time. It was a slight cut on my right forearm. I regretted it after I did it, and then I didn't cut for a few months.

After I had cut the first time, I wasn't happy for what I did to myself. I was disgusted and ashamed of myself. I felt sick every single time I looked at my arm, every time I realised what I had done. To my surprise, that feeling didn't last long and I started to want to cut myself again.

I needed an escape from the feelings of loneliness, worthlessness, and I was truly tired of my life. I started to find other ways to cut myself. I would continue to use the blades from shaving razors and pencil sharpeners. I got addicted to cutting my arm, I enjoyed the release. I enjoyed the physical pain and how it masked my emotional pain. I cut myself on and off for about 4 years. I stopped cutting when I was 19. I didn't want to harm myself anymore. I wanted to try and find ways to cope with my emotions instead of just masking them.

I went 14 years clean, something I thought only early this year that I would never repeat again. How wrong could I have been? I made a huge mistake and I honestly can't believe I did it again.

After being clean for so long I absolutely hated myself. I look now at my hip and my arm and I hate it. I did so well to keep away from the temptation. I guess I could only manage this for so long. It wasn't only this once, I cut myself twice recently. I cut myself because I was in so much pain in my mind that I could not find another way to try and distract this, but it did not help. I did not even feel it. The emotional pain I was in was far too powerful for cutting to take it away. I look at my body now and I think to myself often,

"What have I done? Why have I scarred my body so much?" I know I have destroyed my body. I am covered in scars only to try and help me overcome my emotions.

Many people say scars are signs of battles, battles that I have overcome. I may have overcome these, but the physical scars I have only remind me of the emotional scars, which are hidden deep within myself.

I sit here now and I think how I didn't need to cut. I should have been open about the issues I have had throughout my life; the issues that could have been dealt with many years ago.

Instead, I only bottled up everything and did not even tell a soul. I guess that's the fear an abuser has over you. Knowing that my dad and others would just deny everything that has happened. Why would any abuser own up to what they have done? I continue to occasionally have thoughts of self-harming, but I don't follow it through.

I fight it with every ounce of strength that I have. I close my eyes and think of all the things to be grateful for I have in life. I think about people who I care about, people who care about me. They do not want to see me tearing myself apart. I wouldn't want anyone I care about to tear themselves apart. So, why should I put anyone else through that pain? I will not fall down this route again. I am currently 2 weeks clean and I want to stay clean for the rest of my life.

I have had other issues with self-harm, ones that do not show physical scars. I have made myself sick after eating, in the last few months. I did it because I hated my physical appearance and I didn't want to be known as fat. Every time I would look in the mirror, I would feel disgusted. I didn't want anyone to see how I looked. I would eat something then run upstairs to throw up. I did it for a few weeks.

Maybe it was the sign I was not well, that things were coming to head. I believe there were warning signs early on and if I had noticed them before, maybe I would have spoken out sooner. I haven't thrown up in about 2 months. I only did this as I didn't want to look ugly or feel uncomfortable.

It's something I regret. I have been told by so many people now that appearances mean nothing. It's the beauty inside that counts. I love that saying, but in my head, people's first impressions are formed by what they see. Many people don't give you a chance to get to know you the very first moment.

I know these types of people aren't worth worrying about, but it more common than many people realise. Many people don't like what is different. They don't understand how the person is feeling inside. All they see is physical presence and judge it by that. Of course, many people do not take this approach. They will listen and learn to love you for the person you are, not the person you see. I don't intend on making myself sick again. I don't intend on harming myself anymore. I am going to start loving the person that I am, and I am not going to try and pretend I am someone I am not.

If I talk about today, it's been a good day and I have been out enjoying the sun. I have figured being in the sun is helping lift my mood. I went for a nice 4-mile walk today. It's good to get out. I need this more than I know. I am so fixated on trying to find ways to help me cope that I'm forgetting about all the little things in life that are natural. Sunshine, wind, leaves, flowers, wildlife, and flowing water. These are all amazing natural self-help remedies, ones that are helping me focus my mind on my surroundings and not my thoughts. What helps me may not help someone else, but it may help some. Being at peace with nature helps me, perhaps it can help you too. Try and find that happy place in your mind when you're feeling overwhelmed.

All you need is that tiny little bit of candlelight inside you and you can bounce back from the demons and you can take the fight to your nightmares. Become one with your surroundings, close your eyes, and think of what you have to be grateful for in life. It has helped me greatly.

Before this last week, my mother had not been to Manchester, the last time she visited I was unwell. Much like the time now. Back then though, it was a different version of sickness. It was in February, 2014.

I was sitting at home with Claire, I had worked the previous day and I didn't feel fully well. I was suffering from cold sweats at the time. At home, in the late evening, I had just been playing a video game. I told her how I was feeling incredibly dizzy and my body was freezing cold on the inside, yet I was very hot to touch. Claire took my temperature and it was off the scale. I remember she called for assistance, and before I knew it, there was an ambulance at the house.

I was taken to the hospital. I went for an x-ray straight away; it showed clouding on my lung. I began to vomit; I was put on nil by mouth. I was taken to a ward where I was given all my medications and fluids intravenously. I did not feel right. I was so sleepy, and I was worried what was happening to me. Later that night, I was told I had caught pneumonia and that they would be keeping me in hospital.

Claire left when I was admitted to the ward and went home. Claire visited me every single day, she took the week off work, so she could come and see me. My mum came and visited me, to my surprise. She visited me once in hospital before going home. Dad never came. The last time my dad visited me in Manchester was in 2010, the year I moved here.

What amazes me is that the last 2 visits by my mum were when I was sick. My dad was just not bothered to see me. I kind of like it that way, I don't want him around.

Mum stayed for about 2 hours and that was the last time I saw her. Only until I went to Hedge End to visit her. After spending 4 days in hospital, I was discharged. My friend Greg brought Claire, and they both took me home. I didn't see Leah-Jane while I was in the hospital, she did not come and see me. Claire and I both decided it would be for the best if she didn't see her dad sick. I did miss her so much, the four days I didn't see her were hard.

A few days ago, my mum told me dad hadn't returned home and that she thought he was working at Goodwood.

Yesterday, I asked my mum if he had returned home. She told me he had, but she had not seen him. Why did she not get in touch to inform me that he was okay? I do hate my dad for everything that he has done, but I do not want any physical harm come to him.

I want this to go the right way. I don't want him to run away. I want him to be a man as he puts it and confess to everything that he has done. Apparently, he has not spoken a word to mum in many days. Where does this go now? I need to find the right answer, but do I need to rush this? I really don't know. What I do know is that I need to have a clearer mind and be able to channel my emotions correctly; something I am hoping my therapy will help me with.

Today, on the school run, Claire received a phone call from social services. They wanted to talk to us both and arranged an appointment at 16:30. When I heard this, I immediately felt incredibly anxious and sick. I had to gather my thoughts, worrying about social services wanting to take Leah-Jane away from me. My heart began to race, I just wanted to get this over and wanted to get done with whatever it was to see what was going to happen.

We got home around 16:15. I sat on the sofa feeling anxious, waiting for the phone to ring. When it rang, Claire answered it and spoke to them, then it was my turn. I was told there are no concerns, and they just want me to be in touch if any of us, especially Leah-Jane needs any support. She asked if I wanted to inform the school, but there was not any point as Leah-Jane does not know what is going on and I have never shown anything to her.

I sit here now and I think of my feelings. I no longer have suicidal thoughts; I will not allow myself to self-harm. I feel that my strength is building. I know I need to do the right thing and confront my dad. I know that I need to report all of this properly. I am still holding myself back. I need to be in the best frame of mind, mentally strong enough to face the monster that destroyed my childhood.

I am still that scared little boy, but this little boy is learning to believe in himself. This little boy is scared, but not scared of doing the right thing. I'm hoping that I'll be able to bring myself to open up to the authorities in the next few months. I will continue with my treatment and I will start therapy. I will be better. I will not allow that bastard to take the rest of my life away from me. Living in fear of repercussions that will never happen.

17.9.19 – I AM STILL STANDING!

Someone is staring right into my eyes, through my soul. What is it that its searching for?

Last night I took my sleeping tablet one hour before I went to bed, in hope that I was going to sleep the night. I must have fallen asleep very quickly, but it did not last, like the rest of my nights.

The serpent in my dream had come back, it was stalking me. I could see it staring straight into my eyes. Why do I keep having dreams of this serpent? I know I have to acknowledge the tension in my life. Is the serpent my dad? Perhaps it is, and that, it is trying to take over mind to make me feel fearful. I woke up after it and was startled and feeling anxious.

I felt tired, but I didn't want to go back to sleep. I managed to doze off again only to be taken back to my mum, we were in Eastleigh. She had just paid for a few quid in the slot machines. In this dream, she gambled away all of her money and then asked me to lend her money. Something which had happened in the past. Mum loved to gamble, throwing thousands of pounds into the machines, hoping to win a much smaller jackpot. I tried so many times when I was younger, I tried to make her realise she needed help; help that she never accepted. Mum was clearly addicted to the slot machines.

It would happen every single month, throughout the year. It was clearly always one of the reasons for the arguments at home. Dad hated Mum putting her money in the machines. He hated paying for things alone.

Whenever he figured Mum was gambling, he would become very aggressive. His abuse towards her never helped her come to terms with her addiction, instead, it made her gamble more.

Mum has recently told me that she did it because it was her way of getting away from Dad, that the constant arguments and fights over money drove her to do this. I remember so many arguments over money.

I never had any money as a child. I didn't know what luxury goods were, everything we owned was basic, non-branded products. I don't ever recall even having any shower gels. It's crazy to realise all the small things in life we have now are always taken for granted; the things I own now. The things I can do daily now, I could never do as a child. When I think of this, it breaks my heart for I was neglected in such a way.

Today, as I sit in my room early morning, I feel low. I was so hopeful for a great sleep last night that I feel an overwhelming emotion of disappointment. I look back to my life and find many days I had disappointed my own self. I look at my scars, I think about my memories. Disappointment shouldn't be something new to me.

In my childhood, a time came when I felt upset and disappointed. It was when Mum was making dinner, I was around 8 years old. I remember being really excited for dinner because Mum was making one of my favourite meals, mac and cheese.

I was really hungry because I hadn't eaten any breakfast or lunch that day. I remember sinking the aroma of the meal as it was cooking. It felt delicious and I couldn't wait to eat some. As Mum was getting ready to serve the meals, Dad began to shout at Mum. He had no reason for his anger, he just became extremely aggressive, telling Mum she was

"fucking useless and wastes all the money".

It worried me because Dad didn't cool down. Many times, Mum told him to fuck off. She just quietly began to serve the meals, but Dad picked up a plate and threw it in the pan, ruining the dinner Mum was cooking. Mum got really upset and tried to walk away from Dad, but he continued to shout, telling her he was going out. He put on his coat, sat on the sofa for about 10 minutes, and just fell asleep.

Mum was too upset to cook another meal that day. Dad just slept. I went hungry that day with no food. I was disappointed that we couldn't have a meal together, I was upset that Mum was upset, and that there would be no food tonight.

I look back at that moment and I know that is something I could never do to anyone. Depriving someone of their meals because they are too bitter in their own mind disgusts me. Maybe dad didn't realise that he would stop us all from being fed. Perhaps he was too embroiled in his own rage to realise what he was doing.

Dad was always very selfish. I don't think he has ever put anyone first in his life. He has always made sure he is the one who is noticed. He is the one who is loudest, and he is the one who will always get his own way. This makes me wonder, how do I make him listen to me when I need to confront him? He has never listened to anyone before and the denial will kick back in. Or, he will say he was doing it to make me a better person.

Lorraine was also not fed well; I cannot remember her eating anything as a child. I just don't recall seeing her eat dinners. It makes me wonder if it was the reason Lorraine used to get up in the night, go downstairs, and eat food from the cupboards. She would eat anything; it didn't matter if it was just butter.

I remember how angry Dad would get when he would figure Lorraine had eaten his food. His temper would explode, and he would scream, shout, swear, and threaten to hit Lorraine. Lorraine didn't understand what he was saying. She just saw someone who looked really angry and who was shouting. She always looked so terrified when he did this. Dad was never, not even once, sympathetic to Lorraine, he clearly did not understand her learning disabilities. To this day, still, he threatens to hit her.

However, only recently, I was told Lorraine was doing the dishes and rinsing the plates. He told her

"every time you turn that tap on; you lose a meal." My mum was disgusted to know of it, how he dare say that to a special person like Lorraine.

Lorraine always received benefit money from the post

office. Dad would always take money from her, leaving her with nothing for the week.

Lorraine usually wasted the leftover, little money she had in a day. She would run out of cigarettes and that would upset her, bringing a weird change in her behaviour. I never understood why Dad took so much money from her. Why did he need her money?

Then, eventually, with time, Dad decided to take all of Lorraine's money and give her only £7 a day. It was never enough for Lorraine to buy her cigarettes, and she was left with no choice but to quit smoking.

What worried me more, though, was that Lorraine always received £141 a week, yet she was only given £49 a week. I was too young to understand the complexities of this, but now I know that is downright wrong and disgusting.

I understand having to help someone budget their money, but taking their money is not right. I don't think this was ever explained to Lorraine. I know if my grandmother knew, Lorraine's mother, she would feel pissed.

My mum's mother lived in the United States of America, she stays in regular contact. I don't have any memories of my grandma or grandpa as a child. As far as I know, they visited when I was very young. The first memory I have of seeing my grandma, grandpa, uncle, and aunt, was when I went to Florida on my own in 2006.

When I arrived in Florida, I was in two minds; whether to stay in the United States or to return home after 2 weeks. I stayed at my grandparents' house, in a bungalow that was on a small island just off the mainland. The beach was not far and it overlooked onto the Atlantic Ocean. My room was huge and had a door that lead me into the garden. It was an aesthetically beautiful location.

My grandpa was an American man, served in the American Air Force. He used to love writing and was a journalist writing articles for the newspapers. He was a smoker, and he used to love drinking his coffee black and really strong. I remember once he brewed his coffee straight from the jar, added water and drank it. He took me to the Kennedy space centre in 2006, where I got to see the space shuttles. I was always interested to learn about space and planets as a child and this was truly a dream come true.

I am not sure what my grandma ever did as a profession, but to me, that doesn't matter, she has a heart of gold and really cares for her children. She calls me and asks how everyone is, especially Lorraine. I spent a lot of time with my grandma, I would go shopping with her. It was lovely to have a relationship with my family that were so far away.

My aunt and uncle took me to universal studios. This was an incredible experience; I went on so many rides and was having an incredible time. I saw one huge rollercoaster. I tried to convince my aunt and uncle to come on this ride with me, they both refused. And then, I went as a lone rider, and wow I was so glad I did. I managed to cut the queue and the experience on that ride was one that I will never ever forget.

I only stayed in Florida for 2 weeks, I returned home at the end of the holiday. A year passed and my grandma called me and said she would love to see Sabrina as she had never been before.

I took this as an opportunity to go back out to Florida this time with Sabrina, her first experience abroad. Just like mine the previous year. It was January 2007; I was 21 years old and Sabrina was 14. She got her permission from the school, and so, we started to prepare for our trip.

We arrived in Florida and were received by my aunt, who brought us to see our grandparents. Not a thing had changed, it was as if I had not been away at all. My grandpa said

"James, it's like you have never been away," right when I entered the house. It made me laugh because although it had been a year, it felt like nothing at all.

Sabrina was quiet to start with. She didn't know anyone. I guess she felt like I had the previous year, nervous and worried as it was her first trip abroad. It didn't take Sabrina long to settle in, and we had a trip planned to Disney world. It was an incredible experience. At first, Sabrina would not go on any of the rides, she was incredibly nervous, but after a while, she agreed to get onto the rides. She was happy. It was also the closet Sabrina and I had ever been in our lives. It was nice to be out of the house. Far, far away in a new world, worth beautiful weather and incredible scenery. The feeling of freedom was always amazing.

Sadly, this holiday in 2007 was the last time I saw my grandpa, he passed away 4 years later. I regret never going back to Florida, but to other locations. I have not been back to Florida since 2007. 12 years ago. In my head I know it's time to revisit, to go and see my family, to take

Leah-Jane to experience the magic I have experienced in the incredible theme parks, attractions, and historic locations that the beautiful state has to offer. I know my family would welcome a visit with open arms, something that I hope to start planning soon.

Today is Claire's birthday. My mind has been in such a state that I completely forgot to get her a birthday card. I know Claire knew this, but she didn't seem troubled.

But, I know, the pain and the neglect of being forgotten on your birthday. Luckily, Claire is at work today and I have made a huge effort to buy for her a card and wrap some gifts up for her. Claire really has been trying so hard to be supportive and that means a lot to me.

I just don't want her to feel I have let her down on her birthday. I want her to have a nice day, I appreciate everything she does for me and now it's my turn to do something nice for her. I don't want to be selfish. I want to be supportive and I want her to know that I am also here for her, that although I am every day, I can still be supportive, kind, and caring.

I really hope she will like the gifts I have gotten for her and that she likes the card I have for her. Having nothing on your birthday is really tough. It makes you feel so alone in the world as if no one cares. I wouldn't want anyone else to feel that pain.

Today, I was cutting the grass in the back garden when I saw my father-in-law come round with a box. He told me he was setting Claire's birthday present. Then, my mother-in-law came into the garden and told me she wanted to make Claire's birthday better this year. As last year she came home and the house was a mess, the pots hadn't been done which made Claire cry.

I had no idea that this happened. Claire never told me she was upset. When I heard this, I felt awful. Why had I been so neglectful last year? Why did I not realise? I came up with an idea to dig a new plant bed in the garden. I hate knowing that I have upset people. I guess I'm so used to being upset myself it may be second nature for me to not realise that the little things in life can be upsetting. Well, not anymore. I am going to start paying attention to how my actions may affect others. I know what it's like to feel neglected and unwanted. I don't want people who I care about to experience those feelings as well.

I have no memory of my 18th birthday. Isn't that crazy? Most people would remember their 18th birthday for their entire lives. Your 18th birthday signifies the first steps into adulthood, but not for me. I don't remember a single moment from that day. I have nothing to show from my 18th birthday. I definitely did not have a party; I would remember that. I don't think anyone cared that I was turning 18. It was in 2004.

What I do remember from the 18th year of my life was taking out a silly loan on behalf of my mother. I don't know why I did that. I could now get credit and it seemed such an exciting thing to do. The money didn't last long and then I had to pay all that back. Credit cards were an excitement and were store cards. I could afford all the things in life now that I wanted. I could help out Mum by giving her money and buying things for the house, such as an expensive television and furniture. Then, I met the girl who trembled my credit score, worsened my financial situation.

EVERYONE FINDS THEIR WAY IN THE END

Months, or even years, it may even take forever. It took me a while to understand where my life was taking me, and where I wanted to go myself.

I was in a financial hellhole, taking out loans and credit cards to pay off the debt I had. Why did I have to listen to my mum? I was working 52 hours struggling to make ends meet. I was almost paying £2,000 a month off my debts, and they didn't seem to be coming down with the payments.

I was stuck. I didn't know what to do. After the horrible relationship that ended, I had no option. I was stuck, and in 2007, I went onto an IVA to try and curb my debts. It helped greatly but messed up my credit rating. After paying a huge amount to this each month, I was contacted by a solicitor who told me I had been sold this IVA, as I had no assets to protect. The best option was to declare myself bankrupt. I did this in January 2009 and it was one of the most degrading situations I have been in. Allowing myself to financially ruin myself and being easily influenced by my mum's and others to keep buying things with credit and lending money out.

I was discharged from my bankruptcy after 12 months. But this was not the end of it, companies still chased me for money. However, things trickled down and it has since been quiet and I haven't had a debt collection letter in over 15 months. It took me until 2017, before I could use a normal current account again. The banks didn't trust me for the longest time because of my financial past, and well who could blame them?

For 8 years all I could use was a cashpoint card, where I would have to draw money out to buy things. I couldn't do online shopping. I had to pay cash for everything.

My experience with finances has taught me that I must never spend beyond my means. I have learned this the hard way. If I don't have the money for something, I will not buy it. Since I was declared bankrupt, I have been incredibly careful with money matters. Some people would say that I am a tight arse, but I am not. If I see people are struggling financially, I will offer to help them.

I don't want people to fall into the trap I was in where debts spiralled out of control, to the value of £30,000. All this happened in only 3 short years. I have not been in debt since I was declared bankrupt and I have always kept a very close eye on my expenditure. I know what it's like to live each day with no money.

It took me 8 years after my bankruptcy to get myself back on the right track. I now have a nice home. I have clothes I can wear without having to sit in the same clothes for multiple days. I have a nice car. I have all the things that I have had to work so hard to get, and I did this all without having to get into debt again.

If I can fight through the hell of living each day with no money and worrying how I was going to eat and come out where I am now, then anyone can.

People just need to believe in themselves and focus on each day at a time. In the end, the outcome will be positive. I always advise people who are struggling financially to seek help. There is no shame in talking to someone about the daily struggles.

In this day and age, no one will let anyone go hungry. There are so many food banks and the support out there now is incredible. I just wish all this support was readily available when I was growing up. However, even if it was, would I have even known about it? Would I have ever found out?

Mum has always been difficult with money. I remember a few years ago she contacted me and Claire. She told us that the mortgage had not been paid for many months and that she was worried that the bank was going to repossess the house. I asked mum how much money she needed, and she said she needed £1,000 to pay off the debt.

Without hesitation, Claire wrote out a cheque for Mum as we didn't want them to lose their home. Mum always said that she would pay us back. After about 8 months, and many times of asking Mum if she was going to start paying us back, we decided we had enough. She didn't stop excusing us about being skint and not being able to have any money. So, I decided to contact my dad. I told him Mum had taken a loan to pay off the mortgage. To my surprise, he told me he had been paying the mortgage and nothing of that sort had ever happened. He apologised to me and told me that he would make sure we were paid back.

I remember receiving the postal orders a few days later.

Mum was clearly very angry about it and had texted Claire, asking why she went to talk to my dad about it. Mum and Dad had clearly fallen out over this. Mum did not speak to me and Claire after this for several months. I never got the answers from my mum. What did she really need the money for?

She always was adamant it was for the mortgage, but we know that is not true. I honestly feel she gambled the money away that we loaned her. It breaks my heart to know that my mum could do this. She knows how I hate gambling, and she knows the effect it has had on me over the years.

To use our money for her own gambling addiction really upset me. We have not loaned my mum any money since. She has asked quite a few times, saying that her car is going to be taken if she doesn't make payments, but I haven't bowed down. She still has her car, so she must have found her own way in the end.

18.9.19 – BACK TO SQUARE ONE

REST IN PEACE, TONY!

THE YOUNG HAS TO GO, THE YOUNG HAS TO CUT through and fight through, but even then, they can blur from our sights, even with all of the fights.

Another night, another disrupted sleep. I'm beginning to lose count of how many nights it's been since I last slept. I had many nightmares last night, and again, my dad was shouting, telling me how he was going to beat me if I didn't do what he wanted.

"Sort out the garden, if you don't, I'll treat you like I treat Robert", he had said with his eyes ringing ferocity. In my dream, I looked like a young boy who was panicking. Suddenly, I woke up. I felt dizzy, my heart gasping for air to breathe.

I managed to fall asleep again after about 30 minutes, only to dream of falling from the sky. I couldn't see where I was gonna fall, the sight of the ground was blurry as if nothing exists in the world.

It feels I have fallen into a trench, where strange dreams come through like alarms blaring loud in my ears. I'm hoping for my therapy to help me recognise these dreams, to give me the answers I have longed for. I'm not asking for a cure. I just want to understand, after all this time, why now? Why after nearly 3 years of horrible memories have they all come back at once?

I have 3 cousins who I know of. I am sure there are more, but I do not know for sure. Two of them have passed away. They had cystic fibrosis. I do not remember my oldest cousin Kelly. I have seen a picture of myself with her when I was younger. It was a framed photo of me sitting on a toy and Kelly standing next to me. Kelly was only 8 years old when she passed away, it was back in 1989. I have no memory of her. I had just known that she existed. My other cousin Tony, he also had cystic fibrosis. He managed to keep fighting until he was 23 years old, passed away in 2007. Tony had the most beautiful funeral service I have seen to date. He had horse-drawn carriages that went through the streets of London. He was much loved, did so much for his local community. I am so proud of his achievements and what he has done to help others fight cystic fibrosis. The last time I saw Tony was at my grandparents' 50th wedding anniversary, 2 years ago.

I do have some memories of Tony. Back in 1993, I and Robert went on a holiday to Skegness with my aunt, uncle, and Tony. I remember having lots of fun with Tony, we played football on the beach, and we played with dinosaurs. We were both huge fans of dinosaurs at the time because a popular film had released in the cinema. I remember kicking the football into the sea. Tony went to get the ball, but he said something was clinging onto the ball. At the time I was upset because the ball was gone, but when I look back now. I laugh. What could have held onto the ball? A seaweed? It makes me smile, this memory of being careless.

Growing up, my other cousin wasn't so nice to me. I didn't see him much, and he would usually only visit when Tony visited. They would come visit my grandparents with my aunts. He was not polite and used to ridicule me. I was the youngest, and he didn't seem to take a liking to me. I never really knew what his issue was. I remember playing football in the local park. He kept shouting at me, telling me I was crap. He blamed me for Tony's sickness, which really had nothing to do with me. It was Tony's medical conditions, and he would often be sick. I never really liked him visiting. I dreaded him coming to see us. I didn't want to feel sad or afraid of him.

The last time I saw this cousin was in 2016, at my grandfather's funeral. He was a very different person. He didn't say much to me, but he shook my hand, perhaps he knew that he was difficult to me when I was young. Or, he may just be a shy person now. I have had no contact with him since, which to be honest does not bother me.

He is not someone who I would ever really want to socialise with. I guess you could say that I distanced myself from people who have upset me in the past. I guess this is very true. This is probably why I have had difficult relationships in the past and why I had one-night stands after my relationships. I don't think I have ever taken time out to grieve for the loss of people in my life. I just continue to carry on as if there has never been a change.

GUILTY PLEASURE

2008. I was single and I had just come out of a relationship. My heart was broken and I was hurt. I didn't know how to feel. I started using a dating site. I wanted to get back out there and I wanted to try once again.

However, this year, it was not a good year to get into relationships. I went on many dates, but there was just nothing there. I would go on, perhaps 2-3 dates a month. Sometimes we would get on really well, and other times, the dates were just not right. They were quiet, or we just did not have any interest in the same things.

Some of these dates would turn into one-night stands. We would go out for a meal, watch a movie, or even just go for a drink, then I would usually go back to their place. We would sleep together and then that would be it. They would try and get in contact after, but I would just ignore them.

I had 8 one-night stands in 2008. I am not proud of this at all. I hate what I did and how I ran away from what may have been a great relationship. I know at the time I was scared of commitment. I was so hurt by my previous relationships that I couldn't let anyone get close to me.

My trust in women was completely crushed, it pushed me to fall into this rut of guilt and hopelessness. It is hard for me to forgive myself. I haven't told people about my one-night stands because I don't want anyone thinking I just sleep around, that I am what people call a player, because I am not. I was scared of commitment. I was scared of being hurt. I hid away and I didn't want to allow anyone to get close to me.

Came August 2008, things started to change and I went to New York. It was time I made efforts to reflect on how I was behaving, and although I didn't want to get hurt again, I thought about who I may have hurt along the process. I thought about the women I had slept with. I thought about their feelings and I realised I wasn't the only one hurting.

When I came back from New York, I deleted the dating accounts. I also went to Cuba after New York. I took a break to help myself treat my heartache. I told myself I will now wait for the right person to find their way to me. I stopped going on dates for a very long time. I took some time away from relationships to find out more about me. To know what I really wanted in my life?

I know I wanted someone to love me for who I was. I didn't want to rush that. I didn't want to go out and date. I didn't want to sleep with women anymore. I wanted to feel respected.

I'm sure many make mistakes in life. I feel the same mistakes help them become who they are today. I hate hurting, upsetting people. People close to me know this. I have always wanted to be a good man. I have only ever wanted to do good for others, to help, inspire, and to motivate.

I sit and recall people who I have hurt, unintentionally or intentionally. Everyone in their lives can be selfish at times, they may also prioritise their feelings over others. I, too, never wanted to hurt anyone. I would often receive messages after the nights, asking when we would see each other again. Sometimes they would call me, but it would only happen for a day or two. Maybe they were like me, struggling to commit. Perhaps they were, too, scared of getting into a relationship. I just wish I had thought about what I was doing more. It wasn't right of me to fix myself by breaking others' hearts. What I should have done was to take a break.

I have never been able to keep up with people in my life. I have an issue where I tend to push people away when they get too close. I love having friends and my friends know this. They have supported me through all the difficult times.

In the start, it was hard to explain why I had to distance myself. People weren't able to tolerate my mood swings, which ruined the little friendships I had. We would then lose contact and I would feel all alone again.

I wonder why I push people away? Is it because growing up I didn't have anyone? I didn't have anyone to go to? Friendships are hard for me, I don't want to lose my friends, but I'm scared if they get too close, I'll get hurt.

If they ever leave, it will push me to close my heart. It will make me feel very defensive and insecure. I know, for sure, my true friends will wait for me. I know this now, but I didn't know this in the past. I really wish I did, because I know if I had this mind-set, I wouldn't feel as lonely as I do.

I will sometimes become difficult and needy. I will want a lot from my friends. It puts a lot of unnecessary pressure on them. I know that I can be hard and I don't want to make people feel on the edge where they don't know what to say to me. I'm beginning to relax away from this, but occasionally it still happens where I feel that my friends don't care about me anymore. This is when I get in a defensive mode and I will keep asking if

"we are okay?" or

"are we going to be okay?" I don't really want to do this.

I just want my friends close to me, and they are. It just hurts to know that I never really knew what a real friendship was, not until I left Hedge End and moved to Manchester when I was 24.

THE BEST DECISION OF MY LIFE

Moving to Manchester was the best decision I have ever made. I moved to Manchester in February 2010. I moved in with Claire. She was pregnant with Leah-Jane. A few days after I had moved, we went on a holiday to Lanzarote. It was a nice holiday. It rained for days while we were still there. Even though it rained a lot, we enjoyed our time exploring Lanzarote.

We went over to visit Fuerteventura, went up into the volcanos. We pretty much explored as much as we physically could. I have always loved exploring. I like to experience the culture, the environment, the history, and the scenery of all of the countries I visit.

One day, on a hot day, we went for a long walk. We saw this volcano not far from the hotel, a few miles only. We decided to walk up to see it a bit close, when we got to the top, we had a look inside the crater. We stayed up there for about an hour before we decided to head down.

This is where I totally forgot myself, forgetting Claire was pregnant and running down the volcano leaving

Claire somewhere alone near the top. I felt like such a fool. I climbed back up the volcano to Claire and apologised to her.

Our visit to Lanzarote made me learn that I was allergic to fungus. I was extremely constipated and in a lot of pain. We went to visit a pharmacy; they gave me some tablets. The instructions were in Spanish and I didn't ask them anything. I took one of the tablets just after the flight home. When I reached, I fell incredibly sick. I started to swell up and my eyes went extremely bloodshot. I vomited a lot; my temperature went off the roof. I remember Claire calling an ambulance. It arrived very quickly, and I was rushed to hospital. The paramedic was trying to use his phone to translate the ingredients of the tablets. When I got to the hospital, the doctors ran the tests and found an active fungus in the medications. They ran the allergy tests and it showed that I suffered from an allergy to fungus, mushrooms, etc.

I wonder how long I have had this allergy. Was my allergy always there? The tests just show if you're allergic to something, not how long has it been present in your body.

I have been speaking to Mum today. She has told me Robert has agreed to sign over his 33% of the mortgage share to Mum. The mortgage on the house was signed in 2001, 8 months before Robert left. It was a 3-way mortgage between Mum, Dad, and Robert.

When Robert left there was no contact and nothing could be done for the house. It couldn't be sold; no loans could be taken out on the property either.

Robert has now agreed to sign his share over, but mum told me it will cost a lot of money to do this. I knew where this was going in my head, so I avoided the questions about money, only to be told Dad has bought a new tumble dryer for the house.

I told my mum how on earth does he think he can buy forgiveness or silence. She said he hasn't spoken to her. He did it for Sabrina. She then asked me if I had told the social services people anything about the past. I told her I didn't, but I know I will have to at some point. I cannot keep this away forever. The right thing has to be done. Our lives have been damaged, and we must be set free from this hell.

In the early hours of the morning, I will be picking Jade up from the airport. She is finally back from her holidays and I will be taking her home.

Going back to the airport takes me back to the last airport run I had made. It was in February 2009; my parents had just been to Egypt, and they needed a lift home. Their flight was to reach early morning. I lived in Hedge End and I needed to get to Gatwick airport. The drive there wasn't so bad. Roads were quiet and it was a smooth journey.

It was rather a nightmare on the way back. On the motorway, I heard a loud bang. I pulled over to see the rear tyre of my car exploded. It was 03:00 now, what can I possibly do to fix it? I was 70 miles away from home. I rang for assistance and they arrived within the hour. I was thankful to get the tyre changed, but since it was a space-saver tyre, the journey back at 50mph seemed to take forever.

I was anxious thinking what if it happens tonight again? I really hope it doesn't or I will break down in laughter. If it's not laughter, I will definitely be in tears. It would sure be a sign Airport runs are not for me. I am looking forward to this though. It feels like I haven't seen Jade in forever. It'll be nice to see my friend again, even if it's only for a short while. It'll just be nice to have that friendly contact again. I'm looking forward to hearing about her holiday and all the amazing adventures she has been on.

19.9.19 – DO NOT GROW UP, IT'S A TRAP!

If one thing goes wrong, another thing does not have to, do not beat yourself over the unknown.

I didn't go to bed last night. I stayed up and paid attention to Jade's flight. I didn't want to risk being late, or oversleep and let her down. It was 02:10 and I left for the airport. I had never seen the roads so quiet in Manchester. It was a really quiet, pleasant drive. One without any stress or congestion.

When I reached the airport, I got a text saying Jade had landed. I waited for 40 minutes before she came out of arrivals. She had a huge beaming smile on her face and her eyes were wide. She seemed very happy to see me. It was lovely to see her smile.

We then had a cigarette and journeyed back home in Congleton. It was nice to know how great her holidays have been. She had a really good time and that made me feel good. I always told her that she deserved this holiday and that she should have the time of her life. The fact she was so happy, and she had a wonderful time made me feel warm inside.

I dropped Jade back off at her car, and we said goodbye. When will I see her again? I guess I don't know the answer to that, but I am sure we will arrange something soon.

I got back home around 05:10. I was exhausted and I thought I should just stay up because I had to drop Leah-Jane to school. I also had a meet and greet with her teachers. I tried to fight it, but I decided to take a nap at 05:30. I managed to fall asleep around 06:00 only to wake again at 07:15. My body feels as if it is melting inside. Like I have been microwaved. Yet my mind is so active and I do not feel tired enough to sleep.

I'd always advise people never neglect their sleep. Sleep is so important; it helps your body recover and rest. It helps your focus. It's something that I take for granted and so do many others.

I took Leah-Jane to school, there was a short delay before Claire and I could go into the school. When we walked into the classroom I immediately began to feel on the edge. It was a small room full of children with their parents. I could feel my agoraphobia kicking in.

Leah-Jane was sitting at the back, and I was boxed in. There was no way I could get to my exits. My right leg began to tap, which is a strong sign of me being anxious. I couldn't run. I had to stay there. I had to be strong for Leah-Jane. I could not let her down. I wanted to know what she was learning. I wanted to know how I could help more at home.

I was quickly concerned with how they were teaching

the children. Using tablets for homework. I know Leah-Jane struggles with her writing. I was concerned the reliance on digital technology would take away the fundamental skills of her being able to write clearly. I know the age is digital now and I understand that, but I would like for us to continue being humans and not autonomous robots. Humans have been able to write and draw for many millennia. Going all digital worries me. Too much reliance on the world of technology.

Claire raised this concern to one of Leah-Jane's teachers, and I am glad she did. We were informed the tablets are only for short homework tasks, writing is a part of learning in the classroom.

I sighed with relief. It was nice to hear that the world has not gone fully digital yet, and skills we have had since our young age are still of value.

Growing up, I never had a tablet. I don't think they were introduced even in my adulthood. I didn't have a mobile phone, not until I was 18 years old. We had a house computer that was purchased in 1997, but I never really used it much. Technology was very scarce; money wasn't really there to purchase anything at home. I was always scared to ask. Homework was always sent home from school, which was to be completed by hand. I always struggled with this. I never really had any pens; I was scared to ask for them. My homework was usually never got completed. It would just get left until I was in school. This way I could access a pen to complete this. My parents never once asked me about my homework, neither did they ever help me. I remember asking a maths question from my dad. He completely ignored me and didn't say anything. This takes me back to a memory.

I was 6 years old, and I was given a new reading book to learn and read. I remember reading it with my mum. It was about dinosaurs and I loved dinosaurs. I started reading the book well. I was able to get through the first few pages with no issues. I was happy to know my reading was really good. I then stumbled across a tricky word; it was

"roared." I remember struggling to read it and how Mum tried to teach me by

"say roar and red." I was really struggling to process this in my mind. I couldn't quite make out what Mum wanted to me to say so I kept saying roar and red separately. I remember feeling very worried as I just could not read the word. After about 3 attempts my dad shouted at me,

"it's fucking roared, are you really that fucking thick?" I didn't say anything. Dad then continued to shout at Mum, telling her she was wasting her time trying to get me to read and that I was too stupid to learn the word.

I don't remember reading to my mum again after this. I just remember reading books alone in my room. I guess I was scared of what dad was going to say to me if I struggled to read a word correctly. Being told you're fucking useless, shit, and thick had shattered my confidence and self-esteem. I do not like reading out loud anymore. I don't really like reading anymore. I used to love this as a child. It's so sad to know that the love of something you once had can be destroyed by a single person with only a few comments.

People should always follow their dreams. In life, there will be quite a few times when you will see people telling you how you're not good at something. People will always be critical, it's in human nature. We should never take this to heart. We should take it as a way to make us stronger and better at what we love. What's one person's opinion who doesn't like something that I have done? It means nothing.

I know in my heart now if I want to do something I love, I am going to do it. I'm no longer going to sit by and watch the world progress without me. I have already passed on way too many opportunities in my life. I won't pass on anymore. I'm going to follow my dreams.

Everyone should follow their dreams. No one should hold themselves back, put their life on hold for anything. You get one chance in life, make it count. Be proud of who you are inside. Not what you may think you are. If you work hard for something you truly wish for, your dream will come true. I never thought I would go anywhere in life, but here I am, telling my story to bring your true potential to life.

ONE DAY AT A TIME

I am not a literate, overly intelligent person. I didn't do that well in school, but I have done well in life. To live through the abuse, pain, suffering, loss of my loved ones, bullying, and degradation. I have been dealing with a mental illness for years now. Yet I haven't given up on my life. I have tried it in the past, but I don't feel this way anymore. I feel I have so much more to give. We all have so much more to give. There is so much hope out there, for me, for anyone suffering with mental illness and anyone else who wants to have a glimmer of hope in their lives. No matter what, always remember, one day at a time, you can take steps to better yourself and your mind-set.

Growing up, I never had any hope. I didn't believe anything I dreamed of would come true. We never had any money; I was bullied in school. Home was abusive, there was no escape. I thought that would be me for the rest of my life. I always thought I would grow up to be like my father.

I saw from him behave as if he owned the world and it wasn't normal. I hated them. I hated everything. I was so scared of waking up every single day, I never knew what to expect. I was always scared that either mum or dad was going to kill each other.

My fears could have come true only a few short years ago. Mum was working away, travelling all over the country, doing training for health and social care. And while Mum was away, my dad was heard on the phone telling another woman that he loved her.

Sabrina thought he was talking to Mum until she heard him call the woman's name. She immediately told Mum. Mum told me how she stayed quiet, followed Dad around, and finally saw him get into another woman's car once.

She confronted him, but then told me she didn't speak to Dad for a few days. One day, she caught him right then, telling me how he came through the door, and she started to hit him multiple times. She didn't stop. She asked him to get his stuff and fucking leave and never come back. He picked his bag up and headed towards the front door. She didn't want him to just walk away and picked up a kitchen knife. As he was leaving the front door, she raised her arm as if she was going to stab him in the back. She told me how Dad dropped to his knees and said,

"Please god no." Mum said the only reason she didn't do it was because she saw my nephew.

She walked away and let Dad leave. I remember Mum posting all over social media about my dad's affair with this other woman. I know she was hurt, angry, but I really don't think she thought of the repercussions of writing the things that she did.

I remember reading all the negative comments. I did not like what I was reading. I did not think it was necessary to post an incident all over social media. It's something I would never do myself.

Do people really want to read about other's dirty laundry? I know I don't. I had to hide the posts as what I was seeing was making me feel physically sick.

I felt ashamed and embarrassed by how they both had reacted to the situation. I spoke to my dad shortly after this, and he told me he got a horrible beating, but he never once mentioned the incident with the knife. Dad spoke about this for a while as if he was nothing in life but a victim. I guess Dad didn't like being on the receiving end of a beating for a change. Dad rented a flat for a short while, but only for a matter of weeks. Mum allowed him back into the home again and back into the lives of everyone in the house.

When I learned this, I was seriously worried about the impact it would have on my nephew. I thought about the impact the arguments have had on me. How I was so scared as a child and how even now I get scared when people get loud and aggressive. My nephew is autistic, seeing a blade raised towards someone could have long-lasting issues on his mind, issues he may never talk about.

"Why did you even consider doing it?" I asked her.

"I was hurt and", she took a deep breath,

"so angry that I didn't think what I was doing, only until I saw your nephew", she replied furiously. I wish I was there when it happened. I would never have let that happen. Not as an adult.

I saw these arguments myself as a child and knowing how my nephew had also seen this now, it breaks my heart. How many more arguments will it take for them to realise they are abusive enough to stop? How long will they argue before one of them seriously hurts or even kills the other?

Why am I so scared of losing people? Why am I so insecure? Why am I so fucked up? Why is my head always such a mess? I put this unnecessary pressure on my close friends far too often, why?

I'm hoping that therapy will have the answer to this. I am so scared of losing my friends that I go on the defense. I close up, get pushy, and then I make them feel down.

Is this my mental health? Or is this just who I am? Maybe I am trying too hard. My friends have their own lives too, they cannot always be around. I totally understand this. I sit here and I try and find the answers in my head, but I just can't seem to do so. I just start to feel sad and alone again.

I hate arguing, I have seen far too many arguments in my lifetime. I'm worried sometimes that I am acting like my dad. I really don't want to do this. I need to try and channel my emotions. I know that my friends are there when I want them. I cannot keep making stupid mistakes. I cannot continue to be snappy with them. I must change this mind-set or I will end up alone for the rest of my life.

I have felt alone most of my life as if nobody cared about me. I know it's immature of me to trust the person I see when I am at my lowest. I think my mind is conditioned to believe the person I see when I am at my lowest.

I know, for a fact, I was alone all my life. I often find myself questioning if I am alone, in my adulthood, too? And each time, I find an answer that rings in my ear,

"No, I am not alone anymore." Yet I cannot seem to shake the feeling of loneliness and emptiness out of me. Perhaps it's the little boy in me who feels empty, alone, lost, and scared. Maybe if that little boy gets his freedom, his closure, his mind-set may change.

I have so many questions, yet I have no answers. Who holds the answers to these questions? Is it me? I know for sure I will never get any answers from my parents. I will only get to hear things that will upset me. Perhaps, my answers are locked inside my brain somewhere, I will have to look for them.

I sit here and think of memories that return from my past. I am recalling a moment in my life where I was worried about Robert.

We lived in Hedge End; I was very young. I remember Robert telling my parents he had a headache. I remember their response,

"It'll go away on its own."

I remember Robert telling me he wasn't happy, how his headache was bad. Robert walked into the kitchen, and I heard a loud sound. He had climbed onto the countertop in the kitchen, tried to get the medicines out of the cupboard. The cupboard had fallen off the wall, Robert was lying underneath this and all of the medicines were all over the floor.

Dad came out shouting,

"What the fuck are you playing at?" I asked him if he was okay, he wasn't moving, he looked hurt.

Dad then shouted again,

"You are fine, get up and sort this mess out right away."

Though Robert was fine, I just hated how Dad didn't care about him or the fact that he could have hurt himself. Why did my dad not care? Why did he always lack empathy?

WELL, THANKS DAD!

I have never once touched drugs in my life. I guess it's the only thing I can be thankful for my dad. He was always anti-drugs. He always said how bad they were and how you should never use them. I listened to this and I have lived my entire life completely clean, drug-free. Something that I am very proud of.

Going down the paths I have faced in life, it would

have been very easy to turn to drugs for a realisation. I was tempted for drugs; in my head, it was a way to escape the misery and pain I was going through. I managed to fight this, though. I managed to fight off the temptation of taking it.

I wasn't going to give in. I didn't want anyone to be disappointed in me. I stayed strong and I came out a winner. I can understand why people have turned to drugs. Although I have never taken them and I wouldn't know how it feels, but it feels anything like you're away from your feelings and your thoughts. I would never judge anybody who has taken drugs or uses drugs as an escape because we all have our own coping mechanisms.

At times, I did turn to alcohol, which resulted in a few hospital admissions. Two of which were at the national construction college. The first was a night out. I was mixing my drinks. I was 17 years old and I really didn't know what I was doing. The people I were with left me, sat on a bench outside in the middle of a freezing cold itch, in a jeans and a short-sleeved shirt on. I must have been there some time.

When someone came to help, they told me I was that cold, as if you were to pour a glass of milk on me it would have turned to cheese within minutes. I remember sitting on the bench and I remember being in floods of tears. I felt so sick and so afraid. I had been abandoned and I didn't know where I was going to go or if anyone would come and help me. I am grateful to the group of people who found me, got me the help I needed. I honestly feel if help had not arrived that day, I most likely would have died on that bench overnight.

The second time I briefly discussed before. I was in my room and everyone just started to come in. I had a bottle of vodka, and I was drinking it in a mug. The guys were always horrible to me. I drank so much vodka so quickly that I don't remember what happened next. I woke up in hospital with a drip on. I felt awful and very sick. I actually hated the fact that I had woken up. I didn't want to go back to that place again. I didn't want to feel helpless, worthless, and feel degraded anymore. I was sick to death for how those people were treating me, my only escape was to drink alcohol to the point where I was no longer living.

The alcohol would help me forget what was happening at the time. It was a short-term release that helped calm my nerves and made me not think about all the negative thoughts in my head. I would drink excessively, perhaps as much vodka or whisky I could drink until I passed out. I loved the feeling of being unaware. It was a buzz and was my way of coping all of the wrong reasons. I didn't drink every day; I only drank when I could.

I started to realise I was becoming like my dad; a drunk. The realisation hit me like a freight train. I managed to curve my drinking. I did this without support, through my own will power to not become the person I hated so much. I feel this turning point really helped me come forward in life and I have not been drunk in 8 years. I have had drinks, but not been unaware of my surroundings.

I will only have, perhaps 1 or 2, alcoholic beverages if I drink now, but it's only 2-3 times in a year. I think of my family, my friends, and the impact it would have on them if I were to turn back to alcohol.

So many people who I've come across in life have known somebody who suffers with alcoholism. I do not want to add to that stress, I do not want to concern them of my well-being every single day. I know what it's like to worry about somebody who drinks excessively and I would never want someone else to worry for me. Alcohol can destroy lives, it nearly destroyed mine.

THE PENNY HAS FINALLY DROPPED!

It is 3PM, Jade has paid over a surprise visit. I was so happy to see her. She came to give me some things she had picked up for me on her holiday. A lovely cigarette lighter. The most beautiful turtle bracelet I could have asked for and a lovely turtle ornament with two turtles on its back. Jade knows I love turtles and it was so thoughtful of her to bring me those things.

I was happy to see her. We talked for a while, had lunch, and a nice hot drink. It was only a short visit, but one I really enjoyed. I loved how she thought of surprising me, it made me feel a lot better.

Tonight, I will be seeing Greg and another friend. I was invited earlier for a board game night. I look forward to this. It's nice for me to be able to go out once again. I feel so spoilt by Greg and Jade; I love seeing them.

Claire has been supportive, too, she stays by my side through all that I go through. I am amazed at how Claire has been able to put up with me being the way I am. It's a good feeling to know someone cares for you so much that they will always be there for you. This is how I feel about Claire, Jade, and Greg, it's such a nice warm feeling. It makes me feel safe and secure. I am beginning to smile again. Something I didn't think would happen for a very long time.

I heard from my mum again. I asked her if she was okay today. Her response was

"so so", she continued to say how the atmosphere in the house is very uncomfortable. I apologised to mum,

"you have nothing to be sorry for and it's your Dad who should be sorry", she said to me.

I honestly feel Mum does not know she is also responsible for the way I feel. I just never saw this before.

"The penny has finally dropped", Claire had said to me when I told her how Mum and Dad are treating each other the same way. I guess I was blinded and just blamed Dad for everything, but the neglect wasn't just from Dad, my mum also has to be accountable for her part.

20.9.19 – ESCAPE HAS CONSEQUENCES

Your mental strength may leave your body, slowly or all at once, you may want to close your eyes to ease the pain, look through, ask yourself, is there anything you can hold onto?

I went over to Greg's and met him with his friend. We decided to play board games together. My mind, however, was not focused and I really struggled. I couldn't think of anything other than just how much pain I was going through. I really did try and enjoy the game as much as I could, but for some reason, my mind just did not let me. I feel that the night was a let-down because of my own mind not being able to rest and relax. I went home.

When I got to the front door of my house, I realised nobody was up. Claire and Leah-Jane had already gone to sleep, I went upstairs, got into bed, and burst into tears. I got extremely upset, all I could think of was how I should take my life again.

With everything in me, I tried to fight those thoughts. I really did believe I was free from all the thoughts of suicide, but I guess these emotions can come back. I just can't escape from them. Perhaps, time after time, they will just return. I guess there is no real escape from depression. My depressive state hits me so hard sometimes I just cannot do anything. I just do not have the motivation to get up from my chair, get out of bed, or make myself something to eat.

The following morning, it was very difficult. I managed to get up, take Leah Jane to school. When I got home, I let my body fall on the sofa, and it did not move then. I stayed there for over four hours. I stayed on the sofa because I was worried, I was going to do something to myself. I wanted to die again and if I continued sitting on the sofa, it would stop me from doing anything to myself.

But then, I decided to get up and do something; I went for a cigarette, checked my phone for the first time in almost 24 hours, there was a lot of messages from family and friends. I don't want to put them through any pain or misery.

I don't think it's fair to them and I must learn to understand that my actions will always have repercussions on people who care about me.

I really don't want to take my own life, but my mind lingers, it takes me to a dark place. I sometimes think of the rope I have in the boot of the car. I really don't want to do that. I have no interest in taking my own life. I have way too much to live for. I have nothing to gain from suicide.

I got myself a bracelet made which has strength and hope carved on it. I keep looking at the bracelet to remind myself of my inner strength, that there is always hope, that

I am going to get through everything, that I have been through more than this, and I'm going to continue coming out stronger, with each passing second.

I COULD HAVE BEEN AN ACTOR TODAY!

When I was young, I used to love acting. At around 7 years of age, I auditioned for a school play,

"Captain of the Starship Silver Grey." I was absolutely happy when I got to play the role as the captain of the Starship. It was one of the two lead roles in the play.

I learned my lines every single day. I went to all of the rehearsals. I was so happy to be a part of something special. I felt wanted and needed, I felt like I had a purpose. I remember being excited when the day came for the first performance. I could see my mum in the audience. I couldn't see my dad. I guess he didn't want to come.

When I realised I couldn't see my dad, I choked on my lines at the start. I was upset, but I knew the show had to go on. I looked at the others on the stage, I closed my eyes and I went for it.

I acted my heart out over the next 3 nights through all the performances. I felt like I had accomplished so much, only as a 7-year-old kid. I was on stage acting in front of a few hundred people. The show lasted for about 90 minutes. I was so proud of myself; I still am when I look back. To believe that at 7 years of age, I acted on stage for that amount of time amazes me.

Dad wouldn't allow me to audition for the roles around Christmas. He didn't believe in religion or god and told me that I couldn't go to the churches to do the roles. It really hit me back then, because I loved being on the stage. I loved acting and my dreams were being crushed by my own dad. His views were so archaic, but I was just a young boy. I couldn't challenge my father. I wanted to make him proud, so I listened to him and kept out of the way from all of the Christmas performances. But there was one last performance left in me and nothing was going to stand in my way.

I was 11 years old. It was my last year in primary school and the play was

"Theseus and the Minotaur." I was desperate to play the role of Theseus; I wanted the lead role. The day of audition came, I gave it everything I could, with all my heart and soul. After the audition, I felt things had gone badly. I was upset and I knew in my head I hadn't been successful. Two days later, I got called in to see the drama teacher who congratulated me and gave me the role as Theseus. I was so overjoyed; I couldn't wait to go home and tell my parents. I told Mum and Dad who didn't really seem that interested. Well, I wasn't going to let them bring me down. I was happy. I was acting on stage again and I really felt like my dreams of becoming an actor were coming true.

I rehearsed as much as I could. I read my lines, the script 2-3 times a day. I was so confident in my role, at the second rehearsal, I didn't even bring a script. I wanted to make my parents proud of me. I wanted them to see I was an aspiring actor who wanted to become famous.

The day of the first show arrived. I came out on stage and I couldn't see my parents at all. They had tickets, why aren't they here? I didn't let it phase me, I was upset and hurt inside, but people were dependent on me. I performed my heart out to the best of my abilities throughout the first night. The show was just short of 3 hours. I spent most of the show on the stage giving it everything I can.

After the show, I thought maybe they had tickets for the show the next night, which wasn't the case. I performed the next night and my parents didn't come yet again. It was it for me. It ruined my confidence so much.

I finished the show, and after this, I never acted again. I never went for a rehearsal for another performance. Opportunities were there in the secondary school, but because of constant bullying I went through, and my parents not showing up for my previous performance, my confidence was destroyed and my dreams of becoming an actor were squashed.

I look back on it and I reflect, although my parents may have not been there, I am proud. I am proud I was able to do such an incredible performance at such a young age. I do miss it so very much.

FOLLOW YOUR DREAMS, THEY SAID!

Acting wasn't my only love in primary school. I learned to play the cornet, I started it when I was 9 years old. I asked my mum if I could learn to play a brass instrument, she agreed.

The school loaned me a cornet to use and I joined a 2-person special music class after school. I loved playing the cornet and I really picked this up very quickly. I learned how to play various different music. I was happy to know I had a natural talent.

I couldn't practice this at home. Dad wouldn't let me, he told me it was far too noisy. I remember trying to practice some music one day, and he came into my bedroom, telling me to

"shut the fuck up". I stopped playing and I put my cornet away.

He was trying to watch TV and couldn't hear this properly. There was another time, I was trying to rehearse for a performance that I was going to do. He came charging into my room and said,

"if you don't shut that fucking racket up, I'm gonna smash that thing to bits." He then left my room and I cried.

I hated him so much. It's like he didn't want me to do anything and that whatever I was doing was just irritating him. I never played the cornet at home again after this. I was far too scared. I hated the fact that I could not play at home. I used to lie to my music teacher, telling her I had been practising, because I was scared of getting in trouble if I didn't.

When I was 10, we had a school assembly, and I was asked to play a solo performance in front of the whole school. I was nervous as I had never performed in front of anyone, let alone over 500 children.

The music I was asked to play was high tempo and very fast. It was a difficult piece to play, one that I had only played in the lessons twice before. I was meant to be practicing this at home daily but my father would not let me due to the noise. I was nervous as I didn't feel so confident with only practicing the piece twice.

The day of the assembly came. I stood in front of everyone, my heart was racing and then I was told to go ahead. I nervously missed a note. I stopped for a moment, caught my breath, and then just let my heart do the playing for me. It was incredible. I felt on top of the world and I played that piece of music like I have never played music before.

I couldn't wait to tell Mum and Dad what I did and how great I felt. I came home to tell them that day, but they were fighting. Dad was screaming at Mum and all she was doing was swearing back at him. I just went to my bedroom. There was no point telling them. They probably would have never cared anyway.

Sadly, I stopped playing the cornet at aged 11. I was going into secondary school. The music teacher asked me if I wanted to carry on. I told her I would have loved to, but the issue is I would have to purchase my own cornet.

I asked my dad for it; he couldn't even wait for a moment before he said

"no". He said he didn't have any money, and he did not want that noise in the house. It was the last time I played the cornet.

I haven't played any musical instrument since. I have always been scared of making noise as I don't want to irritate people or make them angry. I couldn't be an actor, and I couldn't be a musician. I was so talented. What a different life I could have had if my dreams weren't crushed.

As an adult, it's so easy for anyone to say

"follow your dreams." Everyone has childhood dreams of what they aspire to become, what they want to be. The problem is, in childhood, following those dreams can be difficult if you don't have the support.

I never had the support and I allowed it to crush my dreams. I think every person who has children should help their child follow their own path in life. If their child has dreams, they should help encourage them. I can understand why some parents feel worried for some dreams may not make any money. But they would never know how rich it'll make their child feel inside, knowing that they are doing something they are passionate for.

Money doesn't make happiness, pursuing your dreams and turning them into reality does! Support each other, motivate, inspire, and give all the support you can to make someone's dream come true.

To help someone follow their dreams is the most powerful gift next to loving them whole-heartedly without judgement. To support someone to follow their dreams, by maybe purchasing equipment for them, giving them time, to take them to classes, and supporting them.

It's like the football team, you go and support, you cheer them along whilst providing physical support by being there. It doesn't have to cost money unless the dream needs it for fancy costumes or instruments, then the people around you will find what you need.

I guess as adults it's easy to forget what we dreamed of as a child and the lack of support or the support you have. It's also having the belief and courage in ourselves to strive to be who we want to be. In a recent musical, it became popular as its champions were the underdog. For me, the message is loud and clear; be who you want to be. I say if your inner child still wants a dream, strive to reach it. It may be a massive leap, but we all need a leap of faith in ourselves sometimes.

Having others believe in us is always a bonus, and we need that, as it reinforces our self-worth. To make the dream, become a reality, it's about having SMART targets. SMART targets are specific, measurable, achievable, realistic, and time-bound. This means that you have the building blocks to achieve the dreams you strive for. Sharing your dreams with people who support you means you are more likely to achieve them in reality.

FAMILY TIME

I have been on two holidays with my father, one to Cuba in November 2008, and another to Mexico in April 2009. I was so excited for Cuba, I booked it on a very short notice for 2 weeks.

I went to work and asked my boss if I could take some time off. He said

"yes, no problem." I was so happy. The day came and we jetted off to Cuba. Dad was complaining for not being able to smoke and spending the entire flight making roll-ups. In Cuba, the weather was heated, it felt amazing. It didn't take long for us to arrive at our hotel.

Immediately Dad began complaining his clothes were a mess in his bag, demanding the hotel iron them. He sent all of his clothes away for ironing and didn't realise it left him with nothing.

He went to the bar in just his underpants. He didn't

care, he was not ashamed. I was embarrassed. Every day, he would drink a lot, he would point out women saying

"look at that one." He had no respect for women there.

One day, he was so drunk he stripped off naked in the middle of the day in the sea. The waves of the sea pulled his shorts away from his hands. He then started running completely naked in front of families, children. He didn't care. I felt humiliated. I managed to get his shorts for him, and he was struggling to put them back on.

Three women walked past as he was struggling and started to laugh at him. He made a vulgar comment back at them. I was just too ashamed to be there, but I couldn't leave him. He wouldn't come back to the bedroom. Instead, he wanted to go to the bar to drink more. He would stay up all night drinking. He would just move to the 24-hours bar after the main bar had closed. I would always go back to the room around 22:30PM. He just wasn't interested, told me most mornings to stop being a wimp and stay up drinking with him. I had no interest in drinking. I was on holiday and wanted to relax. He just never seemed to understand this.

I had a digital camera at the time. Dad stripped naked in the room. He was so drunk, told me to take pictures of him. Stupidly, I did this for reasons unknown. I guess I was just used to doing whatever I was told.

The following day, he asked me to delete them when he was sober because he didn't want my mum to know. These weren't the only pictures he asked me to take.

He asked me to take pictures of women; of those who were sunbathing. I did not do this. I couldn't, I knew this was disgusting and I refused. He told me he was going for a drink again.

I am so glad I managed to stand my ground when he asked. He really did not have any respect for anyone. It makes me sick to have this memory that someone could ask me to do such a disgusting thing. I would never expect anyone to be so cruel and disgusting. I am so ashamed of him for asking me to do that, and for behaving the way that he did.

We went on a few trips in Cuba. He behaved himself on the fishing trip and the catamaran. However, when we went into the local towns, he wasn't so pleasant. Cuba is very poor and a lot of people beg for money. Some of them make you gifts for a small amount of money. He would be rude to them. Telling them to

"fuck off and leave him alone." I couldn't believe how he didn't care about those who were suffering. He was so selfish, I understand why people do not give money to beggars, but being impolite, rude, and aggressive is just not necessary in any way.

I do have a good memory from Cuba. It was the first time I drove a speedboat. What an adrenaline rush that was. I was the driver, Dad was the passenger, and we got to take the boat through the mangroves and around some small islands of the archipelago. I loved this moment, how the wind was rushing through my hair, blowing on my face. It was amazing, a memory I will never forget.

Being at sea, being in control of the sea, I felt I was where I belonged. The moment only lasts a few short hours, but it was a moment I'll probably never get again in my lifetime.

Mexico was a completely different type of holiday. We were only staying there for a week. It was in April 2009, and swine flu was making headlines worldwide. I was worried about going, I wasn't sure what would happen or what to expect. We arrived in Mexico and it was incredibly hot. The hottest place I had been to in my life.

The scenery was beautiful, water as if crystal clear. I had never seen such clear water in my life. When we arrived at our hotel, Dad was very angry. He demanded to see the rep. We couldn't see them until the following day.

The following morning, Dad managed to arrange to see the rep. He demanded an upgraded hotel as the hotel we were staying in was not of the standards advertised. Somehow, he managed to get us a massive upgrade to a 5-star luxury resort with a private beach.

The hotel was absolutely incredible, it was out of this world. It was so luxurious, not a spec of dirt anywhere. I didn't even need to move. Someone would come over for assistance with whatever I needed.

Our room was near the top of the hotel. Just outside the room was a view of the bottom of the pool that was on the roof. It was amazing. The room was huge, so many luxuries. I felt like a celebrity, I felt so rich.

Dad wouldn't eat Mexican food at the hotel. The food to me was superb, but he was just not interested. He would drag me to a fast-food chain restaurant daily to get his dinner. He was never really into the culture of trying something new.

I went on this beautiful trip called Xel-Ha, it's a natural water lagoon and oh, what a location it was. It was bursting with wildlife. There were iguanas just roaming around on the paths, eating salads people were throwing at them.

There were so many beautiful birds in the trees. The lagoon itself was connected to the sea by a bridge. This bridge was a floating bridge and moved with the current. It was so much fun to walk across. Trying to keep balance and not falling in was just an adrenaline rush. The sea was so choppy, but the lagoon was so still. It was remarkable to see the two different flows of water just separated by a few feet. I remember jumping into the water and swimming around, it felt so warm. I found a cave, you had to go underwater to get into this cave. I and dad both went in it. It was so beautiful inside, beauty I had never seen before.

The day was so incredibly hot that we had to keep in the water or stay in the shade. Just standing in the sun felt like your skin was going to burn instantly. We jumped off the large, high rocks swinging from the rope into the water. It was such an incredible place to visit. Somewhere I would love to visit again, just to see such natural beauty, it really was an eye-opener. The day ended and we headed back to our hotel.

Many of the places started to close because of swine flu outbreak. Many planes were empty. This was to bring back passengers who were concerned. The local town, however, stayed open as normal. No one seemed to be phased by what was going on around them.

The last 3 days of the holiday, my dad got sick. He said he had a lot of pain in his stomach, and he didn't get out of bed. He wouldn't even go to the bar; I knew he wasn't well then. We had a trip scheduled on a private boat in the evening. He wouldn't go, he told me to go and enjoy myself. I went alone on this trip and it was eccentric, but I couldn't stop worrying about Dad. I was always thinking if he had, too, gotten swine flu.

The day we were leaving, he got himself out of bed. He said he was fine and that he would be okay to travel back home. We got to the airport where we were greeted by staff wearing full-face masks and hazmat suits. They checked us for signs of temperatures, they took swabs of us. It was quite scary as they were clearly taking this very seriously.

We both managed to get through the screening process and were allowed to travel home. This was the last holiday I went on with my dad. I am glad though. I wouldn't want any more holidays with someone who just wants to spend all day drinking.

I have never once been on a holiday with my mum. I have never been on a holiday with the entire family. It just never happened growing up. Lack of money and lack of motivated parents always stopped this. Maybe I should have asked, but what child asks their parents about a family holiday. The family never really spent much time together. If we had a family holiday, I believe without a doubt it would have been a disaster. To be sure, though, I do not know what it would have really been like.

21.9.19 – SILENCE, NOT A NOISE!

Is it that difficult to see and accept rejection? Why are human minds conditioned to react aggressively to rejection?

Last night I took a sleeping pill. I was fed-up of not getting enough sleep, of the nightmares. For the first time in what seemed to be forever, I slept through the night with no nightmares or flashbacks.

I woke up around 09:30AM. I still felt totally exhausted. Had the sleeping pill made me that drowsy? Or was it just my body trying to catch up on the sleep I have not had? Well, it didn't really matter to me. The sun was shining and it was such a beautiful, hot September day.

I wanted today to be incredible, I had finally slept and I had gotten through the night. Today was going to be the day where nothing but positive energy would take over.

I went to get some food shopping. It was quite nice to be out and I bought a lot of healthy ingredients as I wanted to improve my diet. I was in the mind-set that if I start to eat a healthy diet my mind would become healthy as well. I cannot really continue to just pick at food all day. I know it's something I have done my whole life, but things need to change. I need to change to become the man that I want to be!

I had thoughts today about my Dad, specifically of how he hated any noise in the house. I remember playing a game in my room one day with my brother, it was called milk tops. This is a game where you have round discs and you stack them on top of each other. You then have to use the slammer milk top to hit all the milk tops. Whatever milk tops landed face up you got to keep. The winner would be the person who has all the milk tops at the end of the game. We hardly passed 2 minutes playing it when Dad came running up the stairs, he barged straight in my room and snatched the milk tops out of my hand and the ones that were on the table. He said,

"This noise needs to fucking stop! I cannot hear the TV." He then told me that he would destroy them all if he heard any more noise from us.

I was extremely upset with this, Robert, however, didn't seem to care much about it. He just carried on doing something else. I was scared, I was annoyed. I couldn't play anything. I knew whatever I tried to play would make a noise that would just increase dad's anger. I didn't want dad to come upstairs again and start breaking my things. So, I just sat there in silence. I was so fed up there was just nothing that I could do. I didn't want to go downstairs and watch TV with him, of course. He was always rude and ignorant, nothing like a dad should be to his son. I could tell there was no love inside him, there was no kindness. All his day consisted of was watching TV, getting drunk, sleeping and repeating the same every following day.

And I was okay with it because if he wasn't doing any of these, he was starting a fight with Mum. There was a time when I was around 11 years old. I remember it like it was yesterday. Dad was drunk, Mum was trying to go to sleep. All of a sudden Dad began shouting at Mum because she was not interested in having sex with him. Most of the argument's Dad initiated were mainly about sex. He began to become extremely loud. All I could hear Mum saying was shut up. I have work tomorrow and I need to get some sleep. This just angered Dad, all he wanted was to have sex. He did not care about how loud he was or how aggressive he was sounding. The argument would go on for about 30 minutes until I heard Mum shout get your fucking hands off me. I then heard a loud bang. That sound gave me chills. The same moment, Mum came running down the stairs while Dad was standing at the top of the stairs holding his head. He shouted that she had smashed his head against the wall.

I always wondered why Mum did this. Did Dad try to touch her without her consent? I don't know. I guess I will never know the answer to that, not long after the loud bang there was a knock at the door. It was the police, I immediately let them in. Someone had called them due to the nature and aggression of the argument. I never knew who called the police that night, but I am so grateful they did.

One police officer spoke to mum and the other spoke to dad. The police remained in the house for about 20 minutes before leaving. Once the police had left the house, both went quiet for the night. This was not the only argument in my house that involved the police though. I was around 14 years old when one day things became extremely heated after Mum and Dad had returned from darts. It was just another argument regarding sex. But it was a very hostile one as Dad was threatening Mum.

Mum was provoking him to hit her. There was an incredible amount of tension between the both. I was terrified. I came out of my bedroom to see what was going on. They began physically fighting with one another. I was scared that Dad was going to really hurt Mum. So, I picked up the phone and dialled 999. I spoke to an operator. But both of them saw me on the phone at that point and stopped fighting. I quickly hung up the phone to avoid being in trouble. However, after 2 minutes I picked up the phone and the operator was still there. I was scared of them both at that point, so I told the operator that they had both stopped fighting now and everything was ok and I didn't need police support. This was not the case though, they continued to fight until the early hours of the morning. I just took myself to my bedroom and hid away. I couldn't cope with it all anymore.

The cycle of domestic violence consisted of arguing, fighting which gradually stops, and then follows by apologising until it starts again. Patterns of behaviour that repeat until interventions are put in place. The red flags were all there, but none fully got involved with them or me. What we needed was support for me as a child and them.

My advice for anyone in this situation is to seek help. Talk to someone, no one deserves this environment whether he's a child or an adult. What people deserve is a loving, kind and caring environment. Who can you turn to? It should be someone who will listen; a friend, someone from school, work, or even online help or helplines. The important thing here is to speak to someone who can support you and provide you with support / help.

WELCOME TO THE WORLD – LEAH-JANE

It was 2010, I had moved to Manchester, Claire was pregnant with Leah-Jane. Claire was extremely sick for the first few months. She would go through days where there's wasn't a minute of relief, cheese and onion pasties were a pet-hate. Instead, she craved a well-known northern cordial, hot cold, fizzy and sweet flavoured. Soon she became addicted to fruit of any description.

Claire often said she was surprised Leah-Jane didn't come out purple! We did have a scare early on but the scan was fine. Little did I know the reality of becoming a father... The pregnancy went well apart from the sickness. There were no issues of concern. All the scans were good, and we soon found out we were having a little girl. It was mid-July and Claire was now heavily pregnant. We were sitting at home watching a film when Claire went up to the toilet and came back down to tell me that her water had broken. I began to panic and didn't really know what to answer. So, I said can't we just watch the end of the film first. To this day, I ask myself what a silly comment that was. Claire told me we needed to get to the hospital. I immediately got Claire in the car, and we headed to the hospital. When we arrived, we got out of the car. I started to walk quickly, realising that I had left Claire behind me. I turned around and stupidly asked Claire to hurry up. At the time I didn't realise I was being an ass to her out of panic. But today when I reflect on it, I laugh.

When we arrived on the maternity ward Claire was taken straight into the room. She was in labour. Claire refused to have an epidural. She chose to remain solely on gas and air. Claire was afraid of needles and due to her fear, she endured such awful pain. Something I could never do myself.

After a while of the labour Claire had her legs raised and placed on supports. After about an hour Claire shouted that she had a

"fucking cramp in her leg" this made me chuckle and still does to this day. Claire was worried she was going to kick the doctor in the head. During labour Claire was asking the doctor how much it would cost to look after a woman who was having a baby and told them it cost around £2,000 to rehouse a rare newt from one place to another. Claire was asked if she needed the gas or was she just taking it for fun? It did make her feel dizzy and sick.

After 4 hours Leah-Jane started to make an appearance, however, Leah-Jane got stuck during the birth as Claire describes it

"Leah-Jane got stuck in the U bend". The consultant could not get her out. This alarmed Claire and myself. Claire turned and said to me

"please let her be ok, don't let anything happen to the baby". Claire then began to cry and my heart started to sink. I was so worried that something terrible was going to happen.

After a few minutes, the consultant left and came back with a vacuum extractor. They used this to safely deliver Leah-Jane. It felt surreal. Only what I can describe as a frog hopping is how Leah-Jane looked when she was delivered. Leah-Jane flopped out. She was alert and crying this was a fantastic sign. She had a raised lump on her head where the vacuum extractor had been applied. But there she was, a little bundle of joy. A life that I had helped create. I was instantly smitten by such beauty. I was over the moon. I just wanted to take my baby home. Claire and I were silent for ages. We just kept staring at our beautiful little girl. We wanted to clean her up. We wanted to get her dressed.

We wanted to hold our baby and never let go. Claire after giving birth had noticed the mess of blood and immediately wanted to clean it up now that Leah-Jane had been delivered, been fed and dressed. I had already noticed this but I decided to opt to not tell Claire. I didn't want to cause a panic or worry Claire. Claire did manage to get in the shower shortly after. Which she always says was the best shower she has ever had.

Once Claire was transferred to a ward, I went home to get some rest. It was early morning. When I got home, I had an instant upset stomach. I was a father now. I had clearly, accomplished something magnificent. I had the ultimate purpose in life. To raise someone, to give unconditional love. To be an amazing father. Not to be like my dad, but to be like me. To give hope, inspire and show her the way of life without making any decisions for her. Leah-Jane has turned into such a beautiful little girl now, she is my pride and joy. I could not be more proud of myself for giving her the freedom and opportunities in life. Which I will always continue with. I haven't forced her to do anything or stopped her from making any noise. I don't want her to hate me like I hate my father. I want her to love me, which she does.

After three days, I was able to take Leah-Jane and Claire home, I was so happy my family was altogether in our own home. I felt complete. It did not take long for the house to get busy. My mum came to visit, Claire's parents came to visit and other friends. The house was so incredibly busy. Claire was exhausted, I was exhausted, yet we were overwhelmed by guests. Then there was a knock at the door. It was the midwife. She came to check up on Claire to see how she was doing. She said she needed to take a blood sample from Leah-Jane. Claire was reluctant at first as Leah-Jane was settled in her arms. But then agreed. The pinprick to the bottom of Leah-Jane's foot woke her up and made her cry. This really upset Claire and Claire began to cry also. The midwife then asked how Claire was feeling down below and if there was any bleeding. In front of 10 people, the midwife asked Claire if she could take a look. Claire took offence to this and said,

"no thank you, I have just got my dignity back". I felt upset, how could a midwife not be discreet, asking such a personal question in front of so many people. She left shortly after, then so did all the visitors. It was nice to finally put Leah-Jane in her own Moses basket, and nice to get some, much-needed, rest for myself and Claire.

In my own experience, having a child is truly one of the greatest gifts that life can give. You should always cherish your children, give them the love that they need and want. I couldn't ever dream of neglecting Leah-Jane in the way that I was neglected. All parents should put their own children before their own feelings and desires. We were all children once, and we should remember how we would have liked to have been treated as a child. Many people have had fantastic childhoods. Yet many of us haven't. So many children have been mistreated, abused, raped by none other than their parents.

Living in fear, starving and not knowing what love feels like. These children grow into adults who could go so many ways with their lives, drugs, alcohol and suicide, the list goes on. But this should never happen. The inner child that is trapped inside always needs to be released. So many people wait until their abuser has passed away before they speak. But to me, this is an escape for the abuser. All abusers should face the consequences of their actions in their lifetime. Not only in the afterlife. Speak out, talk, and find someone you feel comfortable talking to. You'll always be surprised how many people will listen. Don't be like me and leave it inside you for too long, it can destroy your life. However, it isn't too late for me either. There is still time for me to do the right thing. To prevent further heartache and abuse to happen to my nieces and nephews. I don't know what truly goes on in that house anymore.

But I honestly doubt much would have ever changed. Tonight, I will not be taking a sleeping tablet. I only have one left and I will be saving that for when it is needed the most. I am going to try and sleep naturally. I feel a bit better today.

We had a lovely visit from a friend and her children. It

was nice to catch up as we all had not seen each other in a long time. She didn't know about how I had been feeling, or what had been going on. Yet she was very supportive and caring. Another fine example that people do care. People will listen, it's a case of finding the inner strength inside to be able to talk. So many people struggle to talk, due to shame and the stigma attached to mental health. Times have changed. So many famous people are talking about mental health, I never thought I would have the courage to open up and talk about my troubles. Yet here I am pouring my heart out. It's never too late. It's ok to not be okay.

It's okay to be scared, it's okay to struggle. But you don't have to do this alone. I am no longer doing this alone, I can't. Holding it in any longer would have probably killed me. The feeling of relief from just talking to someone feels like the world has been lifted off your shoulders. I will continue to talk. I will continue to fight.

22.9.19 – THERE'S GOOD IN ME

I GOT OUT OF BED AND CAME DOWNSTAIRS AND watched two films. My mind was alert, but my body was exhausted. I went back to bed around 04:30. Claire was awake and Leah-Jane was in my bed. I spoke to Claire and told her that I am not safe in my dreams. Claire told me that she is here to protect me and that there is nothing to be afraid about. However, when I am asleep there is no one to save me. Am I scared to sleep? I think I might be, scared of what to expect, I don't want to feel unsafe anymore. I am not even tired now. How my mind can just work an overdrive without a break is beyond me.

I guess this takes me back to when I was young. I was never really a good sleeper. How could I even sleep with the constant fighting and arguing? I am always told that sleep is very important. I do strongly believe this. It helps your mind focus and rest. I just wish I didn't have to put up a fight for this. I read somewhere today that depression and anxiety can lead to memory loss. I really do wish I lose the memories I have. Unfortunately, I have a photographic memory and I remember absolutely everything that happens. Is this a gift or is this a curse? At the moment it felt like I was cursed.

What have I done in my life to make me feel the way that I do?

I have discussed how I was never wanted at school, about how I was bullied, that no one wanted anything to do with me, other than to insult me, tell me I was smelly, ugly and poor. I wasn't wanted for anything unless I was useful. When I was in school, I was a very fast runner. I would win the races in PE comfortably. This meant that the team would want me to partake in sports day and their relay races. Being naïve as usual, I agreed to it. All I wanted was to be a part of something and I just didn't want to feel isolated anymore. The day came and it was the 100m sprint. I stood at the start line, and I was very confident that I would win this race. However, as the race was about to start, another competitor told me to get away from them because I stank. As the race started, I just pulled up and pretended to have torn a muscle on my quadriceps. I didn't want to do it anymore. I pretended to limp off the track and sat down.

I was asked if I would take part in the relay race. I said no, I just sat there and waited for the day to end. They only wanted me around as I would win points for the team, not because I was liked or wanted. I went home that day, and I was asked by my dad what had happened. I told him I injured myself in the race. All he said was ok then, he didn't really show any care or concern for me being upset or hurt. I wasn't even hurt, but only I knew that. I put the limp on for many days, so I wouldn't have to go to school. I just wanted to keep myself away from that place.

I guess this does not help my insecurities as an adult and why I question why people only keep me around because I am convenient. I know this is the case with my family and my friends, but others I just feel use me to help aid them with what they want. I shouldn't feel this way. I love helping others. I will go above and beyond to help someone with what they need. I guess maybe I just want the same back every now and again.

Witnessing all the violence at home would at times make me an angry teenager, I was angry with all the fighting, I was angry with all the bullying at school. I would start to punch the walls in my room. I once punched a hole in my wardrobe door as I was so hurt inside and I needed to release some tension. I never displayed anger in front of anyone. I used to hide myself in my room and shove my face in pillow and scream. I would snap pencils; I would even throw things. I look back on this and see a very troubled young boy who just needed love and support from someone. Whether it was from his parents, a teacher, a friend or just simply anyone. I remember hurting my hand once by punching it into the wall. My knuckles began to swell very quickly. I believe it was a foolish thing to do as it still hurts sometimes especially when the weather turns cold. I stopped reacting aggressively towards myself and the things in my room when I realised there was no point. It did not have the power to solve anything. Maybe it was a way of getting it all out instead of just taking all the abuse that I usually did; seeing all the horrible things that happened at home.

Even now I can get argumentative, which I absolutely hate about myself. I do manage to calm myself down, but usually, that is after I have become emotional. I don't hit anything anymore; I haven't done that in 15 years. But I can become loud, something that my dad was like. When I see myself getting upset, I think about how he hurt me. This will stop me and I will always apologise to my friends and family when I act this way.

I have spoken to many people recently. I tell them short parts of my life and what has happened. They always say to me,

"How can you go through all of that and still become the man that you are?" I never truly understand that statement. How do people see me? I don't see me as a decent man. I see myself as someone who is troubled, struggling and has to overcome huge obstacles. I am not an icon; I am not famous. Maybe they see the good in me. Maybe people see that I have a kind heart. I am glad people see me in a good light. I would hate to be known as a monster.

WHERE'S MY CHILDHOOD?

When Sabrina was about 3 years old, she was sitting in my room with me. My Dad was watching sports in the living room. He was shouting at us because he couldn't quietly watch the TV. I had enough of him. I couldn't even play anything with my little sister without him shouting at us. So, I told Sabrina to go and tell Dad he is a monster. Sabrina agreed, went in to the living room. I was standing in the doorway of my room, I wanted him to know she thinks of him as a monster. She told him exactly that. He shouted at her, telling her not to say that.

He then called me into the room and shouted at me very aggressively for provoking Sabrina. I know what I did was wrong, but all I wanted to do was be a child. All he wanted to do was watch TV. He made me sit on the chair in the living room in silence for about 2 hours, punishment for what I had done.

I don't remember any of my parents playing with me as a child. I cannot even ride a bicycle; I was never taught. I once asked my parents about this, they told me they tried to teach me, but I just kept putting my feet off of it.

I have no memory of this or ever trying to learn to ride a bike with them. I still cannot ride a bike to this day. Not something I have told many people. Would I like to be able to ride a bike? I would love to, but now I feel I am far too old to learn this. I feel that as I am getting older, the ability to learn skills are diminishing. I was never taken swimming; I never had a swimming lesson. The only swimming lessons I had were in school. I left school being unable to swim. In the end, I taught myself as an adult.

I try to remember playing board games with them, any games really, but there is no memory. There are small memories of going to the park and playing on the swings, but this was very rare and never happened much. We never went out on family walks or any family days out really. They just didn't exist. Most of my childhood was spent locked up in my room with nothing to do, no one to talk to. The first time I went to an actual theme park was in 2007 when I was in a relationship. I had never experienced a real ride before. Yes, I had been on small carnival rides, but nothing extravagant. I guess so many people in poverty wouldn't know these luxuries that I talk about. But not even a day as a family. No meals around a table, not doing anything together due to the nature of Mum and Dad working, drinking, and gambling.

I look back to being at home all the time, not going out, not doing anything, not making friends, and not talking. I look to now and I see that these behaviours still transpire. I can just sit indoors all day on the sofa and not move. No TV on, no music on, nothing. I feel I do this because it's what I always used to.

It's only recently that my family and friends have made me realise this. It was just a habit and one that I want to rid myself of. I now go out for walks again in the day. I walk to the shops. I put some music on to help lift my mood. Yet there are still the days where I trap myself indoors and isolate myself from the rest of the world.

I am hoping therapy will help change this habit. I don't want to feel like a prisoner anymore in my own home and in my head, because I am not a prisoner, I am free.

When I grew up, I learned driving. I had the freedom to get out of the house and drive wherever I wanted. But I didn't do this. I tried to go out a few times, but I was always asked by Dad

"where are you going, what are you going to do?" I would sometimes say I was just going out for a drive, but then his response would be,

"you're just wasting petrol and money".

Going out, this really put me off. I didn't want to keep answering his questions all the time. I hated being questioned, I just wanted some privacy, to go out and do what I wanted to do without fear of him ridiculing it.

I did manage to get out a few times, I went on a few dates and I would take myself to the cinema, upon return he would be questioning what I was doing, why was I home so late, who was I with. He even once asked me after my date,

"Was she fit?" I just ignored him. I didn't see the same girl again because of his insensitive, vulgar remark. I was 21 years old at this time, who was he to question what I was doing?

I just couldn't bother listening to his bullshit, so I would just continue to drive to work and home and that would usually be it. Unless of course, he wanted a lift, which was quite regular.

Dad didn't drive and needed lifts quite regularly to get to work, or to take him fishing. He would ask me to do this a lot. I guess it was never a waste of petrol to shuttle him around. It was only a waste if I wanted to do something for myself. I believe this still goes on. Instead of me, he uses Sabrina's husband to help get him around. He has always been reliant on others, never reliant on himself. He would be the first person to criticise someone. But could never take the criticism himself. I always find people like him irritating. If they want to be critics and tell everyone how to live their lives, then they should be able to handle the same responses back. Nobody should ever have the right to tell someone else how they should live their life, but unfortunately, the world does not work this way and this happens a lot. Many people want to just own your life.

My Dad has two other kids; they are much older. The last time I saw his first born was in 1995. He was my older brother, I remember him as a tall, very handsome, and very confident person. He came down to see my dad on his birthday. Mum had gotten in contact with him and asked if he would like to join, he accepted. He brought his girlfriend with him, a very pretty, jolly woman. Dad was surprised to see his son; I was surprised to see an adult man who was my father's son when I was only 9 years old. The first thing my dad did was take him to the pub. They spent the whole afternoon, evening, and most of the night drinking.

They came home drunk, I don't know what happened between my dad and my oldest brother, but something must have. The following day he left and has not been back in contact since. That was 24 years ago. Where he is now, I don't know? What happened between him and my dad?

Something my dad knows, and that I will never know.

Mum once told me Dad used to see him when she first met him and they used to play football together. Mum tells me how Dad was rough towards him; he would keep kicking him and knocking him over. Did the abuse start before I was even born? Did it start with his previous two marriages and his son before then? It does make me wonder. Why would he kick and trip on his own son? To me that is Dad showcasing his control and his authority, wanting his boy to be the best at football. Something Dad always wanted me to be good at.

My dad also has a daughter, he has always been open about this, how he got the woman he had an affair with pregnant. Dad told me he has no idea where his daughter is, or where the mother of his daughter is. He has always said the last time he saw them both was when his daughter was 10 months old.

45 years have passed since. I often think of my older sister; what is she doing, she doesn't even know I exist. She never knew who her dad was. I only know her first name, but I cannot find her. I don't know her surname. I don't know where she is, but it would be nice to find her. It would be nice to meet my brother and sister who I know very little about. I would love to know how they are. How their lives have turned out. I doubt this will ever happen; the chances are so uncertain. I have tried to locate them in the past, but I have not had any luck. Maybe one day they will get in touch with me? It's a hope, a thought, but one that sadly does not feel like reality.

23.9.19 – MOM, DAD, I'M HURT!

I LOOK BACK AND THERE IS NOTHING, SUPPORT, LOVE, acceptance, who took my share? I was not deserving of it, I reason, but it is a lie.

Another difficult night, another night with poor sleep. When I was dozing off to sleep, Leah-Jane came running through the door. The sound of the door swinging open sent me into a panic. It took me straight back to when Dad would just barge his way in and start shouting.

I remember shaking, I was sweating heavily and my breathing became erratic. It was only Leah-Jane coming in, but it felt like I was that child again hiding in his room, waiting for the inevitable. For him to come in and start shouting, threatening to hurt me, and actually hurting Robert. I struggled to get back to sleep after this. I could not rest my mind; I eventually did drop off in the early hours of the morning. Only to have more dreams of horror, filled with violence and suffering, yet again.

I was 7 years old and I really wanted to watch a movie at the cinema. Mum had promised me for weeks that she was going to take me to the cinema. I was so excited; the day came and it was early in the morning. Mum started to hesitate and told me that Dad was not very well and asked if we still should go. I told her she had promised me for this movie for so long, that she would take me. Mum kept saying how Dad was sick and he needed her at home. I begged her to take me. She finally agreed and I was over the moon.

We left a little late and got to the bus stop, we managed to get the next bus into Southampton.

When we arrived at the cinema, we were already a few minutes late and had missed the first 15 minutes of the film. I didn't care though. I was at the cinema this was the first time I'd had ever been to a cinema. I was amazed at how big the screen was and how incredible the movie that I was watching was. After the film, Mum wanted to get home very quickly. We did this and I was happy. I got to see the film I was desperate to see. Sadly, this was the only film that I had ever seen with my mum. We never went back to the cinema and my dad never took me for any movies, ever.

I was in secondary school. It was an English lesson, and we were asked to complete a presentation on a piece of music that we liked. We would have to bring this music on a CD, then play it, and describe why we liked it so much. When I heard this, I began to panic. We didn't have any CD's at home. We didn't even have a working CD player. What was I going to do? I spoke to the teacher and asked them if I could opt out of it as I was not big on music.

It was a lie. I loved music but just didn't have much

access to it, let alone any CD's. I was informed by the teacher that I would have to do this, that I cannot have any excuse. When the day came for the presentation, I sat in my room, thinking how I could get out of school. I went upstairs and threw myself down the stairs, to hurt myself, so I didn't have to go. I didn't want anyone to know that I didn't have CD's. I would have just been bullied, called poor again and again. I just couldn't face it.

I told Mum and Dad I had fallen down the stairs, that I had hurt my back and my arm. They didn't seem interested at all, that I may have actually hurt myself. However, my plan did work and I didn't have to go to school. I just went to my bedroom and hid in there for the day. It amazes me how Mum and Dad took no real notice that I could have actually been seriously injured.

I recently fell down the stairs in 2015 and I broke my forearm. Leah-Jane had left crayons on the stairs and I did not notice. Claire was genuinely concerned, took me to the hospital right then. Turns out, I had broken my forearm. Why did my parents not care all those years ago? Why didn't they take me to the doctor or hospital? Our daughter fell off the swing in our garden, Claire took her to the hospital as a precaution, because she was worried. Where was the concern, the worry for me, all those years ago?

I was in my first year of secondary school. In the French lesson, I was given a textbook. I was told it would need to be covered and personalised, so I went home and I found some dinosaur paper. I still really liked dinosaurs. I covered the book really well. I was very pleased with what I had done.

A few days later, I could not find this book. I pulled my bedroom apart in a panic. I kept checking my school bag. I just could not find the book, and I was beginning to panic. I went to the French lesson and informed the teacher I couldn't find this. She was suddenly very angry and started shouting at me in front of the whole class, telling me that I needed to find the book or my family will be charged for a new one. I went home to look for it again. It wasn't anywhere, so I assumed maybe it had been taken from my school bag by someone else or dropped somewhere.

The next lesson came and my teacher noticed I still did not have my book. She became mad at me and told me that I need to bring the book in and losing it wasn't acceptable, or I was to pay for a new one immediately. She then wrote out a bill for £2.50 for a replacement book and told me to take it home to my parents to pay. I took the note to my dad. He looked at it and told me he was not going to pay that at all and that I needed to find the book. I then went to Mum to ask for help.

She also told me she was not going to pay for it, but would write a note to my teacher saying perhaps it was taken from my bag. I started to feel better as I knew this may help. I went back to school the following day; I went into the French lesson and handed the letter to my teacher. She opened it up, and immediately in front of the whole class started shouting at me. She told me not to be so ridiculous and that there is no way that my book would ever be taken from my bag. She continued to shout at me and the other children started to jump in saying

"James, you are stupid".

I felt so humiliated and upset. She then told me to leave the classroom with her where she took me to an office. She told me she was going to call my parents and demand the money. She attempted to call the house, but no one answered. At this point I had given up, I didn't tell Mum and Dad about the reaction and neither of them asked if the situation had been resolved. Luckily though I was given £5 by my aunt, from a Christmas card I had received. I took this £5 to the school and gave it to the teacher where she said to me

"see, it's not that difficult, is it?" I didn't say anything. I just shrugged my shoulders. She handed me a new textbook and told me to make sure that I didn't lose this one or I would have to pay again.

The humiliation from the shouting in front of the class was horrible. It made me feel so small. I never want to feel that kind of humiliation again. I feel teachers should be supportive to their children, not abusive and demanding.

I sometimes think about people, what are they doing now, people who were horrible to me. I just wonder how their lives turned out. Do they ever regret what they put me through? They probably do not even remember me, but to me that is a good thing. I wouldn't want to give a second thought to anyone who has given me a hard time, put me through hell. I will never see any of them again, that I am grateful for.

The move to Manchester took that physical part of my life away from me. The security I felt when I moved away was intense. I no longer had to sleep with one eye open. I just worry about what is happening there now in my absence. I am sure my mum would tell me, but I just can never be sure.

When I was 16, and I was working in the kitchen with my dad, I managed to save some money. I really wanted to buy myself this new games console that had come out. When I got paid, I realised I had the money to do this. So, I went out to the shop and I bought it. I was so happy when I got it home. I immediately started playing games on it. Mum thought I was just buying myself a DVD player, but that was never my intention. I knew I would get shouted at for spending £300 on a games machine.

When Mum called to ask me what I got, I confessed.

She then got very angry, shouting at me telling me how I had wasted my money. I was offended because I knew about her gambling habits. I got so upset that I told her I would just return it. I called the shop and asked them if I could return the machine. They told me that the policy doesn't accept returns unless the product is faulty. I knew the machine wasn't faulty and I started to panic as I knew Mum was not happy with me. So, I told them it was faulty and the disc tray was broken.

Then, they asked me to bring it back to the store, and they would have a look at it. After the phone call, I opened the disc tray and pulled it hard snapping one side of the tray. Now, it was really broken. I took the long walk back to the shop and told them that I was returning it due to it being faulty. They had a look at the machine and told me that I was eligible for a refund.

I was shattered, it was my money I had worked so hard for, yet here I was, returning something I was enjoying just to please someone else. It was only a matter of weeks before Mum started feeling guilty and told me to go and get one. This time I didn't hesitate, I went and got another machine, one that I held onto for many years. I didn't earn a lot of money in the kitchen. I was only paid £3.80 an hour. It took me a lot of hours to work to earn this.

I also had to pay Mum £200 a month as soon as I started working. This was Dad's order and I understand that I should have to pay rent, but sometimes my wage would only be around £250 a month depending on the hours I worked. Did my mum use the £200 to help pay the bills? No, she instead gambled my money away in the slot machines.

They didn't stop for money to pay off the rent. Although they knew how heavy of a debt I was in. Most of the debt I was in was down to them and even then, I still had to pay £200 to Mum.

There was never any financial support. I struggled so much with my finances that I would have to go without food, new clothes, even toiletries. I honestly do not think I'll ever get anything from them.

To be honest, I don't want anything from them. I have never had anything from them anyway. All I ever truly wanted was a loving family. A compassionate, sympathetic, and caring family. I never got hugs off Mum and Dad. I was never even told I was loved, not even as a child, only now as an adult and in the last year Mum told me she loves me. I believe that is because she knows how unwell I am, and deep down, she knows she has a much bigger part to play in my mental health than she realises.

We all feel emotions, this is not a bad thing. Everyone can get angry, sad, emotional, and the like. We need to learn how to embrace our emotions. Without emotions of any kind, what are we, merely objects with no will power?

There is nothing wrong with being over sensitive, wearing your heart on your sleeve, feeling angry, or bitter. It's natural and something every one of us does on a daily basis. We all need to learn to channel them, to try and find our way to help create our own positive well-being.

No one person can remain positive all the time. Even the most positive of people will have their days where they feel down, fed up, and lonely. Negative emotions can drive us to despair, especially if we don't feel the positive emotions. When I start to feel low, I try and do something that helps focus my mind. Maybe it could be going for a walk, drawing a picture, writing your feelings down, sometimes it's the small things that can help. I bottled mine up for too long, they were there and I never did anything to fight them. I know now that was the wrong thing to do. Always remember to talk, if you don't have anyone to talk to, then call a support line. There is no shame in this. I have done this and the people who are there are fantastic. They don't judge, they don't shame, and they listen.

The biggest question I have been asking myself is, why? As much as I want and need to know and understand this, sometimes there isn't an answer. For me the young child/adult didn't do anything to be feeling shame, to be neglected, or bullied. The why is hard, but sometimes, there isn't an answer, it's just because it happened. It helps with recovery in the learning process. I am beginning to realise who I want to be as a human being, a father, a husband, and a friend.

I now make a habit of trying to eat healthier, trying to exercise more, a walk clears your mind, and the rhythm of a walk can help. I've started an app, learning to meditate it helps focus on other things, I've a gratitude diary, two short sentences each day, but you've to focus on the small things. I have bought a bracelet with a saying on it. These are small things that help support me. When I'm having a bad day, I reach out to those close to me. If I needed further support, then an app, website, or a helpline; all are within easy reach.

24.9.19 – I AM NOT AFRAID!

WAS IT MY SLEEP, OR WAS IT MY FEAR? IF I FACE MY fear, will I make it out of it?

I don't want to continue worrying for my sleeping pattern. I am constantly overthinking about the idea of sleep, which is definitely affecting my sleep. Today, I am going to try and stay positive. I will try and stay strong. No more overthinking. No more fear of negative dreams. I must stay strong; I must face my fears. This is something I know I can win and win, I will!

I think now, have I ever faced my fears? I look back on a memory, I have faced my fears head-on. When I was young, I had arachnophobia, I was absolutely scared of spiders of any kind. It was because of my mum I feared seeing spiders. She was so terrified of spiders she would scream at the sight of any spider, no matter how big or small.

I grew up in absolute fear of spiders until I was about 19 years old. I didn't want to be frightened anymore, I went out to a pet shop and I got myself a Chilean Rose Tarantula. It was a safe species of spider to own for a beginner. At first, I was so hesitant to buy this. I remember taking it home, kept it into a cardboard box. I set up its small habitat, opened the box and dropped the spider into its habitat and quickly closed the lid.

I was so scared for the first few weeks that I did not handle the spider at all. As time went on, it begun to grow on me. One day, when I was cleaning out its water dish, it scurried past and brushed against my hand. I quickly pulled my hand out of the tank. I then realised it wasn't painful, nothing had happened. I put my hand back into the tank with my palm facing up, after about 5 minutes, the tarantula walked onto my hand and just stayed put. And there I was, holding a very large spider and I wasn't afraid of it. It didn't feel horrible. It felt good, it wasn't trying to hurt me and I wasn't trying to hurt it. After this, my fear of spiders was gone. Sadly, I gave away the tarantula 2 years later, as the women I was living with would not allow me to keep it in her home.

My mum definitely did not want this in her home. Luckily, my partner at the time found someone to take the spider, and it went to a lovely, caring home.

Facing my fear was always so difficult, but I managed to do it. It took me a very long time to understand what to do, but in the end, facing my fear helped me overcome what I was once so terrified of. People who have phobias are not wimps, cowards, or anything else. They are people who need support and help. People who probably don't want to have phobias or fears. It's always good to support someone through their fears and not let them be scared on their own.

Today was a really positive day. Jade came to see me, it was so nice to see her smiling today, she came over, and we had some breakfast, watched some TV, and she helped set up my new phone, showed me how to use this properly. We then spoke for a while which was really nice, we then decided to go for some shopping. It was amazing. It was great to be out shopping with a friend.

I got myself a new outfit and a new cover for my phone. It was a lovely shopping trip that we really both enjoyed. It was nice to do normal things with a friend, instead of being tucked up in the house all day whilst Claire is at work and Leah-Jane is at school. Jade has been so supportive of me and that is something I will always be eternally grateful for.

MOMENT OF A LIFETIME!

Love knows no boundary, knows no restriction, your love has to move mountains, help someone in need.

In January 2009, I started talking to Claire online, we spoke on and off for about 3 months. In March 2009, we began to speak every single day. Either online with a webcam or talking on the phone. I would sometimes be talking to Claire online on webcam and I would call her and see her eyes roll. She would then smile when she knew it was me who was calling her.

We continued talking more, and we then set up a meeting. Claire was living in Manchester, and I was living in Hedge End. She agreed to take the long train journey to come and see me. I met her at Eastleigh train station, in July 2009 where I picked her up in my car. Something that both she and I think probably wasn't the smartest move. Claire stayed for 2 days before travelling back to Manchester. The 2 days were so much fun, we went to Portsmouth harbour to see the old battleships, we went and looked at so many historical places, and it was a surreal stay. After this, we decided to see each other every weekend, alternating the travel arrangements, so we took turns.

It was November 2009, I received a call from her, and she told me she was pregnant. I had only been seeing Claire for 4 months. I was initially stuck for what to say, but it didn't take me long to ring my parents who were in Jamaica at the time. When my dad answered the phone, he asked why I was calling him, I told him Claire was pregnant, that he was going to be a granddad, and I was going to be a dad. His response was, it's too early in the morning, tell me about it when I get back off my holiday. I was devastated by this because he clearly did not give a shit about this, and he just wanted to sleep off his hangover.

I knew I had to make changes in my life. I couldn't continue to live in Hedge End, I asked Claire if I could move in with her. Claire agreed and I made the move to Manchester in February 2010. We got on very well and I managed to start work 2 weeks after Leah-Jane was born in August 2010.

We updated the house; we decorated all the rooms and bought new furniture that was needed. We cleared out a lot of old items in the house that were no longer needed.

The relationship was very strong, I was very happy and so was Claire.

I was a dad and I wanted to have a proper family. We got Leah-Jane christened on 2011 which went well, she was given her godparents and it was so lovely to have the family together. The christening was at a lovely old church. The godparents were Michelle and Greg, two good friends of mine, Claire's brother, Paul and Jo, Claire's best friend. The post christening meal was at a local pub which has a homely feel and served a good buffet. It was very busy with a lot of Claire's family. My parents came up for the christening. My mum did not take well to Claire's mum, she has mentioned this a lot of times because she felt disrespected at the christening.

I wanted to give Leah-Jane and Claire the family they deserved, so I went and bought an engagement ring. This would be my second engagement, I proposed to Claire on Christmas Day, 2011. Claire said yes and we were both happy.

We looked at weddings for a few months and realised that we didn't want a big fancy wedding, just something small and intimate. We wanted a nice, quiet wedding. So, we opted to have a wedding abroad. We looked at so many locations such as Greece, Dominican Republic, before finally deciding on Cuba. Our wedding was planned, and we offered a few different dates and it then was booked for April 2nd, 2013. We reached Cuba 8 days before our wedding. The weather was amazing, the people were fantastic, and the resort was so beautiful.

We started our holiday normally, just like we would normally do, relaxing by the pool, sunbathing on the beach. Just a normal family holiday. Before the wedding, we needed to make sure all the documents had been received such as birth certificates and copies of our passports. We had to confirm what music we wanted and the type of flowers for the bouquet.

As time drew nearer for the wedding, nerves begun to set in. We did invite both of our parents, but they all declined to come to the wedding, due to it being too far for Claire's family and too expensive for my family.

The day of the wedding came. I had to get ready extremely early and leave the room. It was a hot day, and I was sitting out in the sun, in my wedding suit. It wasn't the most comfortable of situations to be in. I stayed in the foyer; I was waiting to be called to take my position under the gazebo. I got the call and I took my place. I was standing anxiously and I started to look around my surroundings. I was told to stop looking around and just face forward.

When I heard this, I knew it was time. Then, the music started to play, and there she was, Claire was in her wedding dress, holding Leah-Jane's hand and carrying some flowers. She was smiling. We then stood together in front of the Judge. Yes, a judge, a judge covers the weddings in Cuba. He first talked in Spanish and then in English. We exchanged rings whilst we made our wedding vows. We both signed our signatures, then the witnesses did. Our witnesses were staff who worked in the hotel. The hotel staff had been amazing, one of the ladies from the Kids club even helped Claire with her make-up. When we had signed the wedding register, there was a huge round of applause from guests who had been watching, guests that I didn't even know where there. It was surreal, not only was I a dad, I was now a husband too. I had responsibilities and I had to start to shape my life.

After we left the gazebo, we were taken to a horse and cart, where we were given a tour of the area and a photographer took photographs for us. The photographer kept saying

"kiss, kiss." The pictures are stunning and you can feel the love shining through. The wedding was beautiful, I was so happy. The tour on the horse and cart was amazing, although Claire did catch her dress in the wheel of the carriage.

When we got back to the room, it was decorated so beautifully. The room was full of petals all over the floor and there was champagne.

We had our wedding meal at the restaurant, it was lovely, and the cake was so huge we had to ask to share it with the other people in the restaurant. Leah-Jane had ice cream all over her face, but she was still so adorable. A few days after our wedding, we returned home to a living room with gifts from Claire's parents, it was so thoughtful of them to do this for us.

When we were home Claire and I decided that it would be nice if we held a wedding reception, for everyone who could not come to our wedding. We invited all our family and friends. We found a beautiful old stately home and hired the venue. I arranged for the catering and set this up. Claire arranged a DJ, an old friend who she once worked with. My aunts came from London and my parents came too. The reception was incredible. Everyone had a fantastic night and everyone behaved themselves which was amazing.

I tried to socialise with all the guests who were there that night. I went outside to have a cigarette and I noticed my mum standing alone looking angry. I asked her what was wrong, and she told me that my family had all come up to see me and I should spend my time sitting with them. It made me feel low, I wanted to go and thank everyone for coming, not just attend to my immediate family. But I was so annoyed I just pleased my mother and sat with her and my family for the rest of the night.

THE FUTURE IS NEAR!

If I don't move now, I will be held ajar. I have to move into the future I want. I must do it now.

I sit here sometimes and I think about the future. I often wonder what it holds for me, where will I be in a years' time, ten years' time. I know I don't want to be in the mind-set that I am in now. I know that I want to look back on myself and be proud of who I am, proud of what I have achieved and proud that I have been through the darkness and came out on top. People tell me they are proud of me all the time. I hear this from Claire, Jade, Greg, and others.

But first, I need to be proud of me. I need to feel that inside. This is what I hope my future holds. For now, I should stop focusing on the future, the what if's, etc. I should focus on each and every single day, one at a time. I still sit here and wonder who I am? A question that perhaps very few people can actually answer. And I know that the answer is inside me, it's inside all of us. We just need to find this out, one day I hope for this to happen.

I sit back and think of the times when I was a child, and I was nosy; I would sit in the living room with Dad watching TV. I would sometimes ask questions if I didn't quite understand what was going on. I remember doing this with so many TV shows and films, his usual response. Watch it and work it out. As a 6-year-old child, understanding adult TV programmes was never easy.

I would sometimes get lost in the story and not quite understand what was going on. Especially if the past was fast and there were a lot of actions. I guess dad was always too occupied in what he was watching to even try and explain things to me. He hated it when I asked about sports. I didn't understand the rules of football, cricket, rugby etc. I had no real knowledge and when I would ask these, he would get very loud. He would tell me to shut up and not talk whilst he was watching his sport.

Dad wasn't the only one who was difficult with watching TV when I was about 7 years old, my brother put a horror film on. This horror film was about a man who went around and killed children in their dreams. I watched the entire film with him and it absolutely sent me into distress. I was screaming, I wouldn't go to sleep. I didn't want to go to sleep. I was so scared that this man was going to try and come into my dreams to kill me. I thought it was all real.

It was an 18 rated film, full of violence and murder, it was truly horrible. The distress I was in was noticed by Mum who asked me what had happened to me. She was very angry and gave my brother a severe telling off. The following day, he was not happy at all with me and didn't speak to me, telling me that I shouldn't have told Mum. I watch this same film now, and I laugh, it's full of comedy. But only as a child did I think it was terrifying, only as a child when I didn't understand it, it messed with my mind for weeks.

25.9.19 – WAS I ALWAYS LIKE THIS?

If I don't stop my heart now, it will just stop.

Another difficult night, no sleep, it seems as if it's a rule now. I woke up at 03:30AM, I stayed awake until it was time to get out of bed. The morning was typical, just another September day, cloudy and moderately warm.

This morning, my chest was beating fast, thumping so hard I felt it was going to burst out of my chest. I had to take some medication for this. I began to sweat worryingly I had to change my outfit 3 times. At this point, I decided to go for a walk to the shop to cool off. It did not help either, I just continued to sweat. I came home, stripped off, and got changed. I had to take a second tablet which started to ease the chest-thumping and the sweats.

Was it my anxiety that was kicking in all of a sudden?

I have always had anxiety for as long as I can remember. I have always unnecessarily worried about things, minor things, I used to constantly check the cooker before leaving the house. I was anxious about things being left out in my room; in case they would get broken. I would always confirm that I double, triple checked everything before leaving. Even as a child I would constantly worry about mum and dad, worry about my siblings. Worry about what I was going to have to eat that day.

I still worry now, I worry about my family, my friends, leaving lights on in the house. I often find when I am having bad anxiety, it's like there are two people on my head. One who is completely rational and understanding, and one who is screaming the house down. It's a horrible feeling to have and it pushes me to have uncontrollable tremors on my arms and my hands. It can trigger even when I'm doing something simple like making a hot drink.

I have always tried to follow helpful guidelines on how to reduce stress and anxiety, to a degree, these can work. But it's so hard to find the motivation when my depressive disorder is holding me captive. Sometimes, it feels like that there is no escape from my mental health.

Yesterday, though, was an amazing day. I felt happy, free, and I felt like the old me for a change. But today, I feel low, down in the dumps, alone, tired, scared, and extremely anxious. I try to keep myself out of the spotlight when I feel like this and I like to try and trap myself in my safe zone. The sofa in the living room, I can't stay there all day. I have responsibilities, I have school runs to do, housework, shopping, and feeding the pets. I motivate myself by thinking of all the happy times there has been. Sometimes I feel there hasn't been many. But I most certainly have made some happy memories with my family and friends. Thinking of these memories helps me get up out of bed, get motivated, and do what I need to do.

I guess you could say I am like the boy from Neverland. I use a happy thought to help me get through my day. Every one of us at some point in our lives has at least one happy thought. Try to find that thought and hold it in your mind. See if it helps you like it helps me. I feel when you feel so low, nothing feels worth trying. But, stay above it and give it a try, see how you get on with it.

As a child, I don't have many happy thoughts. But as an adult, I have many. I often wonder how I got to where I am in life. It definitely was not because of the support from my parents, which really didn't exist. They didn't really help me get anywhere in life. I never got any financial support or educational support. It just didn't simply exist.

I went into care work when I was 18, my reason was to save up enough money and buy a car, which really didn't take long as I bought my mum's car off her. I had previously given her money for this car the first-time round. So, I purchased the same car twice. I didn't have this car for long. I had an accident in this car, I was driving at night and the steering rack suddenly stopped working. So, I had a steering wheel with no steering. I slammed on the brakes as hard as I could, but it did not stop the car. It hit the curb on a bend the front wheels lifted off the ground. I then dashed through a hedge and straight into a telegraph pole. The car started to throw out smoke, but there I was trying to get my CD player out of the car.

I managed to get out of the car and I called my

parents. They came to see me. They looked annoyed that I had crashed the car. I explained what happened, but the response was very negative. The tow truck arrived and the car was towed to the front of the house. The car was destroyed. The whole front end had been caved in. I had to arrange for someone to come and collect the car for scrap. I was upset, I was without transport and I had to seek out and spend more money on another car which I didn't have.

When I was 17, I fell into a bad crowd. We would go out and by alcohol usually. We would start by drinking these in the local park in the evenings. I didn't know any better at this point and I had no idea what I was getting myself into. We would spend so much time drinking and laughing. I would often be offered drugs which I always declined. After getting drunk, everyone would become very loud. We used to walk around singing loudly and being somewhat a public annoyance.

Soon after, I realised this was not me, the day they started talking about breaking into shops. It was not what I wanted and I didn't want to be round people like these. I met them for about 2 weeks before I knew this was wrong. I stayed out of all the trouble, and I am so glad I did, otherwise, my life may have taken a completely different turn.

There was one time, though, where things didn't go well. I was with a group of guys who I had met from work, we went out and got a kebab. It was the bonfire night, so we decided to get some firework, which was the worst of our mistakes. None of us knew what we were doing or how to even use those.

We started by setting off some of the smaller fireworks, it went well and was actually really nice to see. We continued eating our kebabs and drinking fizzy pop. No alcohol was consumed that night. Then, one of the guys got the large firework out. We placed it onto the ground. We thought it was secure and safe, which obviously wasn't the case. As we lit the firework, it dropped down and fired straight, exploding a tree and it burst into flames.

One of the guys ran around the fence to try and put it out. Little did he know there was a chain on the other side of the fence. He tripped over and dropped his kebab. We knew we were too deep in the fire. We called the fire department and they arrived very quickly. They extinguished the fire. And then we got the longest lecture in history about being safe with fireworks. It went on and on and on. I am kind of glad they told us though.

Someone could have been seriously injured due to all of us being inexperienced and really stupid. I haven't used any fireworks since then. I daren't, I don't want to put anyone or anything at risk. This is something I have definitely learned from consequence. Don't play with fire!

I have used fire before, but only in an incinerator at home which was obviously safe. It was always a lot easier to burn and dispose of it in the small bins that the council provided. It was always only done safely. I would always give strong advice to anyone. Don't play with fire unless you really know how to. Don't damage the environment. Don't put people at risk. Think about the consequences of your actions.

Tomorrow is another day and another chapter in my journey of self-recovery. The destination is important, but at the moment, the journey is full of twists and turns. These twists and turns are full of the light and the dark. The dark times leave me tired, shaken, and fearful at times and the shadows are powerful. I have experienced the art of darkness and it has affected my mental health and how I see myself.

Yet, my people genuinely, selflessly sent support and light my way, Claire, Leah-Jane, Jade, Greg, and those who I hold dear to my heart. It is this light and support that gives you faith in the potential of human, that there is good in people, and not everyone is neglectful, harmful, or dark.

I am rediscovering myself and my own worth, I know it has to come from within for me to believe in myself and decide what kind of a person I want to be. I know that I want to be a good friend, dad, and husband. I have so much I can give to others and my story is helping my escape from the unknown and hurt, it's helping me release my demons, and the darkness to meet the light.

It is a new day; the sun is rising away in the horizon and I know it's a journey towards something bigger and better. What I have had to deal with will not disappear overnight, but every day, I look for one thing positive that I can hold onto.

I want people to realise that we can make positive changes in our lives, gradually and wisely. It all starts with a happy thought that motivates you to get dressed or do something. You need to build up slowly. Gratitude is a way of looking out for the positive each day, it can be anything you are grateful for today. It can be the roof over your head, clean water. Or you may think what made you laugh today? The food you have eaten? Focus differently each day and look for anything minor, do the bare minimum, but do it with your heart fully invested in it.

For some people, drawing is a way to be more present, colouring too. I was once told to print off a picture and then decide on red for anger, blue for calm, pink for love, green for jealousy. The colours connected to an emotion, you then coloured in the pictures with the emotions you felt the most sometimes, and your picture may be full of red to release the anger. It works for some; you could then scrunch up the picture and throw away as the Buddhists do to clear the thoughts away or burn to release them.

Others may write letters to their younger selves to tell them what they wish they had heard or write letters to the people who have hurt them.... and then burn them to let it go.

Moving forward isn't an easy process, but it is a process and the most important part is to talk to people and not bottle things up. To speak to others, if not ring a helpline, text a support group or access support on the internet, everyone is actively willing to support you. For me, I've learned that there are people around me who love me and walk alongside me on my journey, I'm grateful for that. I know, however, it's my journey and I'm facing the demons and darkness. I am determined to kick off the darkness away from my life.

I couldn't settle down last night. I went to bed reasonably early; I was tired and I thought I would manage to sleep. After lying awake for over an hour, I decided to get out of bed and come downstairs. I made myself a cheese toast and put on a horror film. I feel it's a great way to try and it does help you sleep, but I do not advise anyone to do it. I stayed awake until around 03:00 before I finally fell asleep, only for a few short hours, but it was better than no sleep.

Today is the day of my telephone consultation, we have to see which therapy will work well for me. I am sure there is going to be a very long waiting list and now my only option is to go private. I will wait for the call, which is at 11:00 and I will see what they have to offer.

From today, I am embarking on the greatest journey of all. It is now only about self-discovery, any small step I take now can lead me to a better future, and I am truly waiting for it.

26.9.19 – THEY DESERVED A BETTER LIFE!

I remember living with my parents, I know it wasn't just my siblings and I who were neglected. I remember the pets we used to have, my dogs were always well looked after, but the other pets were not. It all started when my mum got me a water dragon, a tiny baby, and he was called Dino. At first, he was well and active, but soon after he got sick. He lost so much weight, eventually, we had to put him down. I was so upset. It was my first ever reptile. Mum continued to buy herself some pets after this. She had a bearded dragon called Roxanne, Roxanne was a fully grown adult and died within her first year due to her age. I remember mum being very angry, saying how it was mis-sold.

She then bought another water dragon, a bigger female we called Lizzie. At the same time, Mum bought a beautiful red-tailed boa constrictor. In the beginning, these pets were well looked after. Mum would take me to the pet shop to buy their food and bedding and made sure we cleaned them out and fed them as they required it. After a few years of owning the pets, I moved out of home. I went to live with my partner at the time. At this point, the shop where Mum got the pet supplies had shut down and was gone. When I moved back into the house, Lizzie was gone. Mum told me that she had become unwell, and she had found her dead one morning. I was very upset as I had no idea what had happened.

A day after, there was a horrible smell upstairs coming from the snake tank. I went to have a look, when I opened the door, I realised the snake was dead. It was so skinny, nothing like it was before I had moved out. I asked Mum why the snake was dead and why its tank was so disgusting. She said that it had become too aggressive, and she couldn't take it out to clean it.

I always told people that we had to give the snake away as it grew too long. How on earth could I tell them that whilst I was living away my family had neglected this beautiful animal? I don't like lying. Personally, I hate it, but sometimes, I feel I have no choice because of the shame of telling people the truth.

It made me realise how I was the only person to take the snake out of the tank. I was the only person to feed the snake, handle it, and clean it out. I knew then that the pets had been neglected and had been allowed to starve to death. I was so disgusted with what had happened.

The cruel mistreatment of the animals really hurt me. I absolutely love all animals and the fact that I had to deal with the snake that had died really hurt. Mum hasn't kept any reptiles since, apart from some musk turtles which are actually looked after. Any creature, be it human or animal should never starve to death, they should never be neglected. Why do I only blame Mum for this? Well, Dad had never any interest in the pets, and he always made this clear from day one that he would not have any dealings with them. Yet I do feel he is also responsible in a way as he would have known what was going on, yet he did nothing about it.

We also had birds, beautiful exotic birds. I remember these as a young teenager. The parakeet was particularly beautiful. It was given to Mum by the owner of the pet shop as he was shutting down. This bird was 15 years old; his name was Jabba. He was a beautiful deep red with gorgeous colours under his wings. He used to mimic the telephone, which drove everyone mad as you would always be chasing after the telephone thinking someone was calling. He used to love eating red chilli peppers, monkey nuts, and lots of different crackers. I remember coming home from school one day to be told that Jabba had fallen off his perch and had died. I was quite surprised by this as the fall was not that far, especially to be deadly. Jabba, however, was at the end of his life expectancy. Jabba's burial was left to me I was just a young teenage boy having to deal with all of this again.

People should never take on any pets if they don't think they can handle. Reptiles are not toys, they are not pets for beginners. They need a lot of care, not just unnecessary care, it all needs to be correct. Their habitat needs to mimic the environment that they are native too. Research, homework, and complete understanding of what you need to do must take place. These are things my mum never did.

My reptiles are well looked after. I did a lot of research before I bought any of them. They get a lot of due care and attention and exercise. They are not kept in a talk every day; they are allowed out to roam. They are fed and nourished with the correct vitamins. If you are ever unsure of buying a pet, then do not buy that pet. All animals are living creatures and should be looked after as if they any other person in your life. You should be 100% dedicated of what you are buying. Don't make the purchase and allow the animal to suffer. It's not fair.

Why do I blame myself for my own neglect? I was never in control of my own childhood. I couldn't make myself healthy meals, I couldn't go out and buy clothes myself. I was just forgotten and left. I was just left on my own to just get on with life and learn through experience, many of which I want to forget. I know it's not my fault that my parents were more concerned about playing darts, going to the pub, using slot machines, and just arguing all the time. Yet I still sit here and think what did I not speak out? Why didn't I find someone in school to talk to? A teacher, cleaner, anyone. I just carried on with my life with my head held down feeling broken and scared every single day.

Why do I blame myself for the neglect of the pets? I wasn't even there, yet I feel somewhat responsible. I feel I should have been there to feed them. To make sure they were clean, handled, and loved, not just left to rot and suffer in their tanks. If I only knew what they were going through, I would have stepped in and saved them. I would have done something. But I didn't, and yet I blame myself for not doing something that I didn't know about. I need to try and get out of this mind-set and stop punishing myself. I need to focus on what went wrong and how to prevent that from happening again.

THE SIGNS WERE THERE!

If you just offer your hand out to someone, you will know why your life is of value, too. Reach out, don't leave any room for guilt.

A few days ago, I was out for a walk, I came up to a bridge, under the bridge was the motorway, I paused for about 5 minutes and I asked myself

"what if?" I honestly do not know what was going through my mind at the time. I stayed still and then noticed all the beautiful signs that people had created on the bridge. You are loved, you are not alone, talk to someone, people will listen, and people care about you. They were so beautiful. I read every single one of these notes and I walked away from the bridge, knowing that I am not alone anymore and there is always hope.

Whoever wrote those messages are incredible. I think how many lives those people must have saved. It may only be small messages, small notes, but like I keep saying the little things in life count. The people who write these should be commended; they are the real hero's in the world. Hero's do not wear capes. They are just everyday people with big hearts who go out of their way to help someone in need.

If you ever feel that you have had enough and you

can't take anymore, stop. Look around you and see that there are people everywhere. Look at the signs. Don't think that they won't listen or care.

The beauty of human compassion is matchless and the nature of one to help another is one of the greatest feelings anyone can experience. If you ever see someone in need, looking lost, or afraid, don't turn a blind eye. This could be you one day. Support and reassurance go a long way in helping stop someone. Stop the risk of seriously harming themselves. I would never leave another person in need alone. So, let's all stick together, reach out and help that one person who needs it. Let's squash the stigma around mental health, let's show the world people can be caring, kind, and compassionate. Let's help others talk, open up, and share their own stories.

I took the phone call from the support team, I was asked so many questions, and I scored insanely high on the depression and anxiety scale. The mention of post-traumatic stress disorder was also raised. I managed to open up about some of the issues from the past, it was really hurtful as I started talking about it to someone. She was very supportive and told me some of the things I have told her may need to be passed on or raised. I opened up and said I was concerned about the children in the house. I was open about the self-harm, suicidal thoughts, and the attempts in the past. It felt like a burden had been lifted and I have my first scheduled face-to-face meeting to discuss options at the start of October. I feel that progress has started and soon I'll be on the right road to recovery. I told her I want closure; I want to find my happiness. I don't want to be snappy to people who care about me. My family and my close friends.

TIME TO LET GO.

Life is like a see-saw, it goes up in the high and unknown, comes down to the bottom and holds you still. The weight of your guilt will weigh you down to nothing, look through and reach out. Don't let anyone stay stuck in the unknown, don't let anyone move with their heart in their palm, hold their hand tight and pull them out of the despairing rut of hopelessness.

I have finally accepted the help I need. I strongly believe recovery starts when you know you need help. Once you have accepted that you are not well, you are already on the road to recovery. There is no shame anymore in asking for help. I have climbed that mountain, and I am going to do everything that I can to win the war against the darkness. I have one foot now in the light. The rest is about how I take the next step.

I think about all the others in my family who have suffered. I hope that they also manage to find their way to talk about the demons from the past. I hope that everyone is able to move out of the darkness. I never thought the day would come where I would break down like I did. I always thought I would keep this in my head until the day I walk into the afterlife. I guess I was wrong.

No matter how much you try and suppress your emotions they always come and get the better of you. Let them out! Let your emotions be free. Don't suffer in silence, don't hide. Don't be like me hiding under your duvet and being scared of what may happen next.

I would like to thank Claire, Jade, and Greg for all their support, and everyone else who has been so kind to me throughout my darkest days. I wouldn't be where I am without all the help and support.

Putting up with my mood swings and standing strong by my side. If it wasn't for all the amazing support that I have had, I don't think I would be on the road to recovery. I will always be eternally grateful for everything they have done for me. I hope now I can move forward with my life and make new amazing fun memories with them.

I hope Leah-Jane continues to grow as she does. She is such a beautiful amazing little girl, who I know will grow into an amazing woman one day. I now have several paths to walk down. The path I choose will be the right path for me, not for anyone else. This is my path and I need to focus on finding my way. I don't know what my future holds. Does it hold happiness or does it hold more darkness? I guess time will tell.

For now, I want to continue focusing on each day as it comes. I shall now walk down the long road ahead, not worrying, not stressing about where I am going, but by being optimistic about what good can come my way.

Follow your own path in life. Never let someone chose your path for you. Make your own dreams, memories. Live life to the full. Love every last minute that you can. Cherish your loved ones. Hold onto your friends and never let them go. Never be ashamed of who you are. In our own ways, we are all different. As I continue my journey, I hope you continue yours. Stand tall with your head held high. Never give up on your dreams, don't let anyone shatter these for you. No matter what they are. I won't allow this to ever happen to me again, I am going to do everything that I couldn't t do when I was a child. I am going to work so hard to set the younger, inner James free, and I am looking forward to see what the next chapter in my life holds.

EPILOGUE

Since this book has been written I have come to learn so much more. More information about my mother and father, and further details on what went on when we were small children. These are stories that can be shared another time perhaps in the future when everyone is ready to open up about their experiences. I have now decided to make the difficult decision of blocking contact with my mother, following disagreements regarding my father. This led to some very difficult messages being sent to myself which contained very negative comments about my wife Claire who had only been trying to protect me from the negativity that was surrounding me. My father has since been arrested for the sexual abuse towards Sabrina. However, this charge was dropped the following day by Sabrina due to victim's guilt. My father was allowed to come back into the house, but to live in the outhouse. This was when my brother Robert messaged me back. For the first time in 17 years, he had gotten in touch. I, Robert and Ricky all unanimously agreed that we did not want my father in the house. There are too many vulnerable people in that household.

I and Ricky disagreed with my mother over the decision to allow him in the house. But this decision was allegedly made by Sabrina who did not want to leave him homeless. He has since left the outhouse, which I was told by Sabrina in a group chat she created on social media. I still have not made any contact back with my mum since he has allegedly left. I am not ready to, not after the abusive messages that I had received calling my wife pathetic. The toxic nature of what's happened in that house managed to keep me awake most nights. Suffering with nightmares and intense flashbacks. Since all contact with my parents has been broken off, I am now able to sleep and rest and I am now much more able to focus on the good that I have in life. I have Leah-Jane and Claire that's the family I live with and that's the family that keeps me going strong.

On Wednesday 6th November 2019 I travelled to Manchester, there I met my brother Robert. This was the first time that we had met in 17 years, 7 months and 3 days, a day I thought would never happen. It was an amazing day and I got to meet his husband. I was so happy to spend time with both of them learning about them and talking about our pasts and what we have both missed out on in the last 17 years. Before I knew it was early evening. Having Robert back in my life was one of the greatest moments in my life. I have always loved Robert and I will always love Robert. We will be arranging more visits as time progresses, and we will continue to strengthen our relationship as a family.

I am now feeling stronger, and I am much more content in my own mind. I feel now that all of us Robert, Ricky, Sabrina and myself will unite and get the relationships together that none of us have ever had. The future looks hopeful now we are all beginning to break free from the grip of what held us back when we were children. I never thought this could ever happen, I thought that all hope had been lost. I have been given a chance, to repair and build the bond that was broken and destroyed all those years ago. I will work with my brothers and my sister to help bring justice and closure to us all. It has been a very emotional few weeks, but a few weeks that have helped repair the damage to my heart.

ABOUT THE AUTHOR

James Keith is a knowledgeable professional with almost 20 years of proficiency in the healthcare industry. James has always been an activist for mental health due to his own experiences in the field.

James wants people to be aware of how to deal with emotional, psychological, and social well-being issues and how to stop them from affecting their lives.

Follow James at
www.JamesKeith.co.uk

facebook.com/jameskeith86
twitter.com/JamesKeith86
instagram.com/jamesikeith

Printed in Great Britain
by Amazon

84785484R00154